D0928543

CAN OXFORD BE IMPROVED?

For Charlotte

In the hope that one day she feels as much

at home in Oxford as we both do

CAN OXFORD BE IMPROVED?

A view from the dreaming spires
and from the satanic mills

Anthony Kenny
and
Robert Kenny

imprint-academic.com
canoxfordbeimproved.com

Copyright © Anthony & Robert Kenny, 2007

The moral rights of the authors have been asserted.
No part of this publication may be reproduced in any form
without permission, except for the quotation of brief passages
in criticism and discussion.

Published in the UK by
Imprint Academic, PO Box 200, Exeter EX5 5YX, UK

Published in the USA by
Imprint Academic, Philosophy Documentation Center
PO Box 7147, Charlottesville, VA 22906-7147, USA

ISBN 978184540 094 1

A CIP catalogue record for this book is available from the
British Library and US Library of Congress

Contents

The outsiders are coming to teach us how to behave, but they won't succeed, because we are gods... The Sicilians never want to improve for the simple reason that they think themselves perfect.

Don Fabrizio Salina

If we want things to stay as they are, things will have to change.

Don Tancredi Falconeri

From *The Leopard* by Giuseppe Tomasi di Lampedusa

Preface

I have spent most of my working life in Oxford and I am proud to
have been associated with the university and several of its colleges.
I have been saddened by recent months of turmoil there. I know that
many universities in the UK have much more serious problems, but
I have written only of Oxford because that is the university that I
know and love.

Anthony Kenny

I write about Oxford primarily from a commercial perspective. I
have spent my career in the private sector, as a member of senior
management teams, as a consultant and as an investor. As a consultant I have worked for clients as prosaic as a manufacturer of gas
boilers, and as high-minded in their objectives as the Wellcome
Trust and the BBC. I have worked in start-ups where I was one of two
employees and I have worked in a corporation of 14,000. I have lived
and worked in the UK, Sweden, Hong Kong and the US. As a result I
have broad experience of the ways, good and bad, of the private sector, and I hope some of that perspective may be useful.

But coupled with that perspective is a deep fondness for Oxford
and the collegiate university, where all the lower strata of my personal geology were laid down. I have spent 14 years in college housing, a great good fortune. Virtually my entire schooling was in
college schools. I have attended a dozen reading parties in the Alps,
perhaps the quintessence of the college ideal. My first paid employment was returning books to the shelves in Bodleian. I attended the
other collegiate university, and as for many people, to this day many
of my best friends are still those from my college. I was married in
Balliol chapel. Thus any criticisms I offer stem only from a belief that
great though Oxford is, it could be even greater if it would only take
the brakes off.

Robert Kenny

Acknowledgements

Both authors are grateful for help generously given by Sir Martin Jacomb, Simon Jenkins, Lord Sainsbury of Preston Candover, Sir Colin Lucas, and Andrew Graham, each of whom would disagree with a good deal of what we say.

Chapter 1

What is Oxford and What is it for?

The answer to the question set by the title of our book, the reader may have guessed, is "Yes". In the course of the book we argue towards this conclusion by identifying Oxford's present strengths and weaknesses and by canvassing several strategies for reform. In reporting on the present state of Oxford we adopt a fourfold approach, anecdotal, historical, analytic, and statistical. Chapter two records forty years of experience of Oxford from many points of view, from graduate student to Pro-Vice-Chancellor; it seeks to identify, from each of those viewpoints, the positive and negative aspects of the collegiate university. Chapter three describes how the institution appears to a near neighbour. Chapter four narrates the history of previous attempts to reform Oxford and explains how its present institutions evolved. Chapters five, six, and seven offer an analysis of the current relationships between the central university and its constituent colleges, and seek to strike a balance between the advantages and the demerits of the present system. Chapters eight and nine offer an external evaluation of the current financial and organizational structure of Oxford. In chapters ten to twelve we examine and reject three different strategies for getting the best out of the collegiate university: leaving things as they are, imposing reform from outside, and declaring independence of government funding. In the final chapter we offer our own modest proposals for eliminating Oxford's weaknesses and building on its strengths.

But those who make proposals for the improvement of Oxford must first make clear what they believe is the nature of the institution, and what function or functions they believe it serves. This we attempt in the present chapter.

All universities worthy of the name have a twofold purpose: education and the advancement of learning. The primary beneficiary of education is the individual student, the advancement of learning is a benefit to the human race. Education may be liberal and general or it may be specialised and professional; the advancement of learning may take the form of increasing knowledge, as in the sciences, or of enhancing understanding, as in the humanities. Universities differ in the emphasis they place on education and research and the different forms of each.

The goal of a liberal education was stated by John Henry Newman as the production of "a cultivated intellect, a delicate taste, a candid, equitable, dispassionate mind, a noble and courteous bearing in the conduct of life — these are the connatural qualities of a large knowledge; they are the objects of a University"[1] A more recent Oxford man, Boris Johnson, currently shadow minister for higher education, has stated "The main point of a university education is to achieve a personal intellectual transformation, and, who knows, an emotional and spiritual transformation as well. The evidence seems to be that this transformation is, additionally, of huge economic importance." [2] In place of Newman's emphasis on nobility and courtesy, twentieth century educational theorists stressed that universities had a role in the transmission of a common culture and common standards of citizenship in a democratic and inclusive society.

Oxford sets great store by its educational role. Its current corporate plan insists on parity of esteem between disciplines and between teaching and research. "The fact that Oxford attaches as much importance to teaching as to research" it states" is one of the characteristics that distinguish it from many of its international competitors".

Universities may, but need not, offer professional as well as liberal education. Oxford has traditionally emphasized liberal education, offering professional training only in medicine. Unlike many US universities, it has no law school. The studies offered at the recently founded Said Business School occupy a position intermediate between liberal and professional education. Newman, the great advocate of liberal education, was no opponent of universities offering professional education — but he insisted that what distinguished it from narrow training was its place within a broad intellectual context. A university is an empire of many different disciplines, and a teacher in a university "will know where he and his science stand; he has come to it, as it were, from a height, he has taken a survey of all

---

[1]   *The Idea of a University*, ed. I.T. Ker, Clarendon Press 1976, p.110
[2]   *Daily Telegraph*, 6 February 2007

knowledge, he is kept from extravagance by the very rivalry of other studies."

Oxford has never been a merely local university: for centuries it has, with Cambridge, been seen as an institution for the education of the nation. Both friends and enemies describe it as an elite institution. It is not, and should not be, elitist in the sense that it recruits its students only from a privileged class. No one today would say, as Lord Curzon did when Chancellor a hundred years ago, that Oxford had a special duty to educate the leisured classes. Entry to Oxford must be open to all who have the ability to benefit from the advanced education that it offers. Oxford must be elitist in output, not in input. It must educate an elite in the sense that it must produce graduates who are qualified to be national leaders in a variety of professions.

A university education confers on the individual an economic as well as an intellectual benefit, because the lifetime earning power of a graduate is greatly enhanced. The economic benefits of an educated workforce accrue to the nation as a whole, and hence provide one reason why the taxpayer should contribute to the costs of maintaining universities.

Oxford has for more than a century educated foreign as well as home students, and nowadays overseas students make up a large proportion of those pursuing graduate studies. Under the current charging regime, students from outside the EU pay higher fees and therefore help in the funding of the university. But though Oxford has no particular duty to educate nationals of other countries, there are non-financial reasons for welcoming them. British undergraduates benefit from being educated in a cosmopolitan community, and the graduates from abroad make a significant contribution to the university's research output.

The national interest in universities is principally concerned with their educational rather than research function. But, as the corporate plan stresses, research is no less an important concern of Oxford than education. Oxford's international reputation is largely based on its research productivity, which is what places it consistently in one of the top two places in UK and European league tables, and in the top ten of the global competition. Whatever may be the appropriate level of fees for their education, students cannot be expected to pay for their university's research. And we may ask: do Oxford's research activities have as strong a claim on the public purse as its teaching activities?

The advancement of science and learning is an international good which can, in the long run, benefit everybody: but is it important that high quality research should be carried out in the UK rather than elsewhere? It might be argued that provided good research is done, it does not matter where it is done. On this view, national enthusiasm for Oxbridge is not very different from fanatical support for a national football club, and football clubs do not expect to rake in taxpayers' money. Does that mean, therefore that there is no national interest in supporting first class research universities in this country?

We think not, for two reasons, one economic and one moral. The first reason is one that has been much emphasized by governments of both parties in recent decades: university research is capable of being exploited in ways that bring great benefits to the national purse. Universities UK claims that our universities contribute £45bn annually to the economy and much of this comes from research.

The second reason rests on less tangible considerations. If the advancement of research is an international good, then those nations that can support it have an obligation to do in proportion to their means. There is an exact parallel with peacekeeping. International peace is a global good, but one which cannot be achieved everywhere by local effort. Consequently the more powerful nations have a duty, which is nowadays quite widely accepted, to take their part in peace-keeping operations even if these bring no immediate national benefit.

There is a particular reason now why there is a national and international interest in supporting universities like Oxbridge. While, in the light of eternity, it does not matter where scientific insight is gained or where medical discoveries are made, it matters greatly that they should not all be made in a single country. At the present time the evidence seems to show that only Oxford and Cambridge can consistently compete, across the academic spectrum, with the principal universities in the United States. It is therefore in the international as well as the national interest that such universities should continue to flourish.

Oxford is a historic university: i.e. its present value is inextricably tied up with its past record. As a result of its history, it is a collegiate university, containing no less than thirty nine autonomous colleges. The central university officers, such as the Vice-Chancellor and Registrar, have much less power than their counterparts elsewhere.

Only Cambridge has a similar structure, and even there the system is not quite comparable.

It has long been traditional, when explaining Oxbridge to American visitors, to compare the colleges to the states of the Union, and the university to the federal government in Washington D.C. But a rider needs to be added in order to distinguish Oxford from Cambridge: in Oxford, the South won the civil war. In other words, Oxford's structure is confederal, rather than federal.

There is currently a widespread perception, both inside and outside Oxford, that it is in need of reform. In this book we propose to consider how far this is true, and if so what reforms should be made, and how they may be achieved. In particular, we wish to address the question to what extent Oxford's flourishing depends on its unique confederal structure.

Chapter 2

An Oxford Life

I matriculated into Oxford University as a graduate student in 1957 and in 2007 I have just ceased to be a member of its governing Congregation. In the intervening fifty years I have seen the collegiate university from almost every viewpoint except the bottom and the top. I was never an undergraduate and I was never Vice-Chancellor; but I have occupied a score of other positions that gave me an opportunity to survey Oxford's virtues and vices. In this chapter I want to describe how the university and its colleges appeared from these different angles of vision.

I came to Oxford after eight years of study at a continental university, where the principal method of instruction was to offer compulsory lectures to students assembled in a vast aula that held up to five hundred at a time. In comparison, Oxford seemed an academic paradise. Since I arrived as a graduate, I have never received the undergraduate one-on-one tutorials that were, and, are, regarded as the jewel in the crown of an Oxford education. My first encounter with the system was when, as a student myself, I was employed on piece rates by college fellows to give tutorials to their overflow pupils. But graduate classes too were humane and intimate gatherings by comparison with continental lecture courses.

Best of all, attendance at lectures and classes, whether for graduates or undergraduates, was largely a voluntary matter. A lecturer would offer one or two lectures a week during the eight-week terms; for students it was neither necessary to enrol nor obligatory to persevere. For undergraduates it was the weekly tutorial, not the lecture courses, that kept noses to the academic grindstone. A graduate student writing a doctoral dissertation received, instead of weekly tutorials, advice from a supervisor appointed by the faculty. I was lucky in my supervisor, and learnt a lot of philosophy in my two years in residence. Many of my contemporaries, I came to realise, were much less fortunate: graduate students did not have a comfortable niche in the collegiate university.

In 1964 I returned to Oxford to seek an academic post in philosophy, my dissertation having been completed in absentia, examined, and published. Philosophy, then as now, was taught as one of several groups of disciplines making up BA courses known as "honour schools". The two principal ones were known as "Greats", in which philosophy was combined with ancient history and literature, and "PPE" in which it combined with politics and economics. In many colleges there are more Greats and PPE pupils than the philosophy fellow, or fellows, could teach unaided, and to help out a short-term post is created, with the title "college lecturer". Oxford titles are often misleading, and a college lecturer does not have to lecture — any more than a reader earns his keep by reading — but must give his stint of tutorials. Often colleges combine part-time lecturerships to create a single appointment paying a basic living wage and offering free board and lodging. I was given a joint appointment at Exeter and Trinity Colleges, which I held for less than an academic year. The teaching duties were quite heavy, and in my first term I gave sixteen hours of tutorials a week on four or five different topics.

Fellow and tutor

Since a college lecturership is a transitory job, holders are encouraged to apply for long-term Fellowships. A vacancy at Balliol from October 1964 was offered to me early in that year, so that my letter of resignation to Exeter and Trinity followed soon after I took up my lecturership. From the academic year 1964–65 I was a fellow and tutor in philosophy at Balliol. I was appointed by Balliol's governing body on the recommendation of a committee which included, beside the Master and a number of fellows, a couple of philosophers from elsewhere in the university.

Tutorial fellows of colleges, then as now, formed the backbone of Oxford's academic staff. As a member of a college's governing body a fellow, however junior, shares on equal terms the administration of an ancient charitable corporation. If the fellow is also a tutor he is responsible — perhaps with one or two colleagues in the fellowship — for the education of undergraduates in his own particular discipline. Tutorial fellows commonly form the majority of a college's governing body: but there are often fellowships also for college officers such as bursars and librarians, and there are always a number of professorial fellows holding chairs associated with the college.

Tutorial fellowships are commonly linked — either immediately or after a probationary period — with a lecturership in a university faculty. From 1965 I held such a post—known for historic reasons as a CUF (Common University Fund) lecturership. Some two thirds of my salary was paid by the college, and one third by the university; this was a roughly proportionate recompense for giving twelve tutorials a week in college and sixteen lectures a year for the faculty. After a while I was also in demand to supervise graduate dissertations; but this was an optional activity, and I received a modest extra stipend in respect of each pupil.

My situation was typical of the dons in arts and social sciences who made up the majority of Oxford's teaching staff. Colleagues in science subjects had a greater proportion of their stipends paid by the university, and had heavier lecturing obligations; they were called 'university lecturers' tout court, without any reference to the CUF. On the committees appointing to these posts, correspondingly, electors appointed by the university faculty outnumbered college electors.

Setting and marking degree examinations was not part of a fellow-lecturer's duties. It was and is a principle of the Oxford system that pupils should not be examined for their degrees by their tutors. Tutorial teaching is a college responsibility, final examinations are the responsibility of the federal university. This separation of powers has the merit that candidates in examinations have no incentive simply to regurgitate the ideas of their tutors. Moreover it means that tutor and pupil are in alliance together to anticipate and defeat the wiles of the examiners in the Final Honour Schools. At the end of term tutors would wait, with almost as much impatience as the candidates themselves, the eventual publication of the class list.

One of the most significant duties of tutorial fellows was the admission of undergraduates—this was entirely a college, not a university, responsibility. In the 1960s groups of colleges set entrance examinations which formed the principal basis on which candidates were admitted. Tutors also took account of references from school teachers, and actual and predicted performance in A-levels. Every serious candidate was also summoned to an interview by the tutors. In later years, the entrance examination was abolished, because it was believed to favour candidates from independent schools. I am not sure that either the efficiency or the fairness of the admissions procedure was thereby improved, and in more recent years examinations have been reintroduced in some faculties.

When appointed to Balliol I was, as a matter of routine, made a Master of Arts of the university. Becoming a college fellow was one of several ways of obtaining this degree without doing any extra work or sitting any extra examinations. Notoriously, those who had an Oxbridge BA could simply wait a few years and pay a fee. I did not even have to pay a fee, since the college paid it for me.

Member of congregation

It was, in fact, in the college's interest that its fellows should take the degree because that entitled them to membership of congregation, the assembly of all MAs engaged in teaching or administration in Oxford. Congregation was the town meeting of dons; in constitutional terms, it was the sovereign body of the university. Most of the university's executive business was conducted by a much smaller elected body, called hebdomadal council. But any proposed change in the university statutes, or major item of business, had to be submitted for approval to congregation, which met several times each term.

In practice, meetings of congregation were rarely more than formalities. Congregation's official home was a historic and uncomfortable building adjacent to the Bodleian library. It had once been used by King Charles II as a House of Lords, and it served as proxy for the House of Commons in the film *The Madness of King George*. But nowadays it is not large enough to hold more than a tenth of the members of congregation. If, rarely, an issue was controversial, proceedings were moved from the austere Jacobean surroundings of the congregation house into the Restoration splendour of Christopher Wren's Sheldonian Theatre, which could hold eight hundred.

During my fourteen years as a fellow of Balliol I can recall attending meetings of congregation only twice. On one occasion the topic was whether an honorary degree should be conferred on Prime Minister Bhutto of Pakistan. Of more lasting significance was a debate on the abolition of the requirement that all those admitted to the University should have knowledge of Latin. Scientists claimed that some of their best candidates were frightened off by compulsory Latin; for many arts dons the proposal to drop it resembled the sack of Rome by the Vandals. Not only arts dons opposed the abolition: I recall the social scientist Max Beloff thundering, "We are an historic international university, not the downtown campus of the Oxford Tech." But the scientists won the day.

On less colourful issues congregation usually allowed hebdomadal council to get on with the running of the university in its own way. The system was a pretty cost-effective form of democracy,

which did not waste a great deal of anyone's time, and did not inter-
fere much with everyday business.

As a junior working don, I had no direct contact with hebdomadal
council and saw the Vice-Chancellor only from a distance at degree
ceremonies. In 1968 the university administration moved from the
impractical grandeur of the Clarendon Building to premises of utili-
tarian dreariness in Wellington Square. There it remains to this day.
An American friend of mine who visited the Vice-Chancellor there
in the early years of the new millennium said that no head of a grade
school in the US would tolerate an office so cramped and shabby.
The squalor of the Vice-Chancellor's premises was in striking
contrast to the ample elegance of the accommodation provided by
colleges for their heads. But until recently nobody minded much,
because the Vice-Chancellor was always a head of house as well,
with his own lodgings to go home to.

Member of the philosophy sub-faculty

I was involved in university administration at the bottom level, as a
philosophy lecturer. There was then no philosophy faculty, only the
faculty of Literae Humaniores, of which philosophy was a sub-
faculty. Twice a term the sub-faculty met in the evening to discuss
such matters as the subjects to be offered for examination, the
content of question papers and the specification of texts to be read
for them. This was important, since that was the way in which the
faculty, as opposed to the colleges, determined the syllabus to be
followed. The sub-faculty also ran a library, and through a sub-
committee prepared the termly lecture lists. There was an informal
agreement that each lecturer would give one course on a specialisa-
tion that interested him, and another bread-and-butter course (on
elementary logic, say, or the philosophy of Descartes) that was likely
to attract a large audience. In those days there was no feedback about
lectures: pupils' assessment of their teachers was still in the future.
But of course, given the voluntary nature of lectures, they could vote
with their feet.

From time to time the subfaculty would consider vacancies in
existing posts and proposals for new ones, setting a list of priorities
for subject areas to be covered. Such discussions generated much
excitement, but their effect was distant and muted. In order to obtain
funding for the university part of an appointee's stipend, the proposal had to travel upwards through the Lit. Hum. Faculty board to
the General Board, which oversaw all the faculties. The lecturership

would then have to be paired with a suitable college appointment, and by the time an individual was elected to the joint post, college preferences would often have won the day against the sub-faculty's original aspirations. The sub-faculty might have wanted a practitioner of mathematical logic, and the person appointed might turn out to be an expert on Hume.

Other than as a lecturer, there were three ways in which, while a fellow of Balliol, I was involved with the larger university.

First, I had to take my turn as an examiner. Examining for one of the larger honour schools, such as Greats or PPE, was a formidable task which ate into the summer vacation, involving the reading of hundreds of papers, interrogating a number of candidates viva voce and attending many meetings with colleagues to determine a class list. I was fortunate to avoid being called on for a major school, but did my stint by examining in the BPhil (typed theses to read, rather than cramped manuscript) and in the smaller honour school of PPP, in which philosophy was combined with physiology or psychology.

Second, I was for a while a member of the faculty board of psychology itself. My appointment to the board puzzled me, since I know no psychology; but I found that my function was to cast a vote on issues in which the psychologists themselves could reach no decision, being equally divided. Without the presence of the external members, the active faculty found it impossible to set priorities. It was my first experience of the utility of external members on boards.

Third, there was the *Oxford Magazine*. This periodical was founded around 1880 as an independent organ of comment on university affairs. Liberal at first, it quickly turned conservative and at the end of the nineteenth century it was the organ of the Non Placet society, a group opposed to reform of any kind. In the twentieth century it became less partisan, but also less commercially successful and in 1970 it died. Many felt the lack of a periodical for informal debate among senior members, and a friendly businessman was persuaded to fund it for a trial year to get it back on the road. During 1972–73 I was its editor, writing and publishing comments on university topics of the day and uttering mild criticisms of council and the general board. Our issues were generally popular but we did not secure enough advertising to make the journal viable and it folded once more. In 1985 it was revived, funded now by the University and its Press. Ironically, it became more and more critical of the administration's policies, and was the great forum of opposition to

the reforms proposed in 2005–6. Chancellor Chris Patten said that it
was as if the Vatican was funding the *Atheist Weekly*.

College committees

Despite this degree of involvement outside Balliol, most of my
administrative experience during the 1970s was within the college.
Most business was dealt with not at meetings of governing body, but
through an executive committee of a dozen fellows. There were a
number of college offices that rotated among fellows, with duties
attached in return for a reduction of teaching hours. Thus, in addition to the Master, there was a Senior Tutor, a Tutor for Admissions,
an Investment Bursar and an Estates Bursar. The executive committee consisted of these dons, plus a full-time Domestic Bursar, and
half-a-dozen members elected from the fellowship. (Later, for a
period, the committee was reinforced by a number of student officers from the junior common room) It was chaired by a Vice-Master
and worked through several sub-committees: the domestic committee, the estates committee, the investment committee, the library
committee, the eleemosynary committee, and so on. There were in
fact too many committees, which took up too much time. I once
counted 27 different committees; at any hour on a Wednesday afternoon one or other of them would be in session in the college's old
common room under its library. There was even a committee to elect
to committees, known as the nominating committee.

Most colleges operated a similar apparatus of committees, but
there was one feature that was, I believe, peculiar to Balliol. At 6 p.m.
on Wednesdays a time was set aside for consilium, a one hour informal meeting of the fellowship. Any item that, at governing body or
in committee, had shown itself to be seriously contentious would be
referred to consilium. Discussion there was frank and informal, and
would be concluded by a non-binding vote. A straw vote at
consilium would normally be rubber stamped by governing body,
since the constitution of the two bodies was identical. Indeed, I now
recall only one occasion when it was not, and that was at a later
period. When I was Master of the college, I proposed a drastic reduction in the number of college committees. This was passed by
consilium, but when the proposal came to governing body all the
committees were restored.

The Wednesday afternoon sequence of committees and consilia
always ended with a dinner in the senior common room, which was
restricted to fellows and which all fellows were expected to attend.

The theory was that any quarrels between fellows that might have occurred during the conduct of college business would be healed in this convivial atmosphere before bedtime. It may well have been due to the institution of consilium dinner that during my twenty-five years in the college, Balliol was free from the internal cliques and feuds that have sometimes troubled other governing bodies.

In the course of time I served on most college committees, but my main administrative experience was as Senior Tutor for four years. The Senior Tutor was responsible for the academic administration of the college, and he was the secretary of tutorial board. This was an assembly of the tutors, which met thrice a term to take general decisions on college academic policy, and particular decisions about the courses and disciplining of individual students. The Senior Tutor, as the board's executive officer, had responsibility for arranging and monitoring the tutorial teaching of the junior members. In practice the implementation of most decisions was delegated to tutors in individual subjects, and the Senior Tutor only intervened if some tutor neglected to make suitable arrangements.

The Senior Tutors of all colleges collectively formed a committee that met once a term to achieve coherence in academic standards and policies between the colleges, agreeing the amount of teaching to be reasonably requested of college tutors and fixing standard rates for the payment of piece-rate teaching by outside free lancers.

I found the Senior Tutors' committee the most business-like of the various intercollegiate bodies that I have been a member of over the years.

The most important issue facing the college in the 1970s was the admission of women. At the beginning of the decade Balliol like all other colleges was a single-sex institution. Many of the fellows were anxious to be able to admit women to the college, but that required a change of statute, and any change of statute that affected the university needed the consent of hebdomadal council. In May 1972 council put forward a scheme whereby five of the men's colleges should, among them, be allowed to admit a hundred women annually for the next five years. Until 1977 the university intended to "withhold its consent to the alteration of the statutes of any other men's colleges designed to permit the admission of women". Balliol was not among the chosen five, and in an uncharacteristic mood of bloody-mindedness the college considered contesting before the Privy Council the legality of this interference with its autonomy.

In the event the Sex Discrimination Act of 1975 weakened the University's power to control the number of mixed colleges. A free-for-all followed in which all the men's colleges, fearful of losing out to competition during the admissions season, voted to change their statutes. The women's colleges were more reluctant to become mixed institutions, but under the pressure of anti-discrimination legislation all have now done so, the last being St Hilda's, who admitted male students in 2007.

I had not been senior tutor for long when in April 1976 I was placed on the search committee to seek a new Master to replace Christopher Hill who was retiring in 1978. The fellows of Oxford colleges take a very long time to choose their heads. Balliol's statutes laid out in detail a brisk formal procedure for the election of a Master, but for many years the statutory proceedings had been largely a formality. They were preceded by many months of sifting candidates, ending with a declaration by the fellows of the person they intend to elect when the statutes allowed them to do so. Other colleges had and have a similar system. Very rarely, the governing body of a college in the formal proceedings overturns the informal decision, with some of the fellows switching their votes for a candidate other than the one chosen in the straw vote. The rejection, as it were, of a bride who has already bought her trousseau can cause great pain; but no action for breach of promise is allowed.

The length of the pre-election process is not seen by the fellows as a burden; quite the contrary. In the words of Mercurius Oxoniensis, they are not at all reluctant to prolong "the ins and outs of these delicious proceedings". There is a certain satisfaction, if not a very noble one, to be extracted from summoning some London grandee, submitting him to an inquisition by the governing body, wining and dining him to give a taste of the pleasures awaiting an incoming head, and then regretfully deciding that he is not *quite* good enough for the college.

In the election of 1978 it took the Balliol fellows about a year to decide that they wanted to elect a candidate from within the fellowship. At this point I withdrew from the search committee. Having been quizzed by each of the fellows, I was pre-elected in June 1977, and my appointment was duly confirmed in the statutory proceedings in the chapel in the spring of 1978. I took office in October of that year.

Master of Balliol

The Master of a college has little statutory authority. He chairs the governing body and has a casting vote, but the only power he has is the power to persuade. There was a legend that a former Master, Lord Lindsay, after every fellow had voted against a measure he had proposed, closing the meeting with the words "Gentlemen, we have reached an impasse". But I had no similar force of character, and in the course of a dozen years as Master I often had cheerfully to accept being voted down.

In the last week of every eight-week term the Master has to conduct an operation known as "handshaking". (In other colleges a similar institution is known as "collections".) Undergraduates come one by one to sit at the dining table in the lodgings and listen to their subject tutors sitting across the table, as they report to the Master on the term's work. Handshaking gives a head of house an opportunity to check up on the tutors as well as undergraduates. Most pupils were taught personally by Balliol fellows — the college discouraged too much farming out — and it was not too difficult to tell how well a tutor knew a pupil for whom he was responsible. If a tutor made an unfavourable report, a pupil was always given a chance to respond on the spot. A few would seize the opportunity to shift the blame on to a tutor; those who appeared reluctant to do so I would later invite to see me privately, to discover whether they had any genuine grievance.

Even in private, I always found a great reluctance in junior members to complain about the dons; a camaraderie commonly grows up between tutor and pupil. My probing left me with the impression that that Balliol tutors were in general a conscientious lot. Any pressure I brought to bear on any tutor whom I suspected of short-changing a pupil had to be quiet and informal: a head of house has no power to fire or discipline a fellow.

In an autobiography I described the job of a Master in these words.

> A Master of Balliol has to relate to the three different estates of the College: the junior members, the senior members, and the old members. It is one of his duties to try to make each of these groups understand and be ready to learn from the others. I spent much of my time trying to explain to undergraduates why dons think as they do and to dons why undergraduates behave as they do, and to alumni why the College today is not what it was when they were in the heyday of their youth. If I were asked to put the duties of a Master in a nutshell I would say that it is to be a peace-maker: to hold the ring between senior and junior members, to

persuade one fellow that he has not been impardonably insulted by another, and to reconcile old members to the college of the present day. (LIO,18)

A job description today, rather than in the heyday of the student revolution, would place less emphasis on peacekeeping between junior and senior members. It would, however, lay stress on something not then mentioned: the raising of funds for the college. I did in fact, as Master, head a septcentenary appeal; but it took less than two years and for most of my tenure I was allowed to direct my energies elsewhere.

As Master I was of course a member of all the committees concerned with the college finances, meeting regularly with our estate agent and our investment advisors. The college's income derived from three sources: endowments, fees, and board-and-lodging charges made to junior members. At first we were at liberty to fix our own fees, which were paid without question by local authorities. Within a fairly narrow band different colleges fixed different rates, the level of fees varying in inverse proportion to endowments. Under the Thatcher government, however, fees reclaimable from local authorities were fixed each year by the government, and fees for overseas students were fixed at a full-cost level. After an initial sharp drop, the demand to come to Oxford turned out to be resilient.

Theoretically we aimed to balance the income and expenditure of the hotel side of the college, but in practice there was always an element of subsidy. With the cap on fees, and the difficulty of enforcing realistic board-and-lodging charges, endowment income became more important as the years went on, and that was why in 1982–84 we needed a capital campaign to increase endowment by £2m.

The College Contributions Committee

The wealth of different colleges in Oxford varies greatly, and there had long been in operation a system of taxation of the richer for the benefit of the poorer, overseen by a College Contributions Committee which consisted of representatives of the donor colleges balanced by representatives of the recipients. The committee was normally chaired by the head of a college in the middle of the league table, to hold the balance between the other members. Balliol, with an annual income of about £2m, was neither rich nor poor, and I was asked in 1987 to chair the committee, and to review the whole taxation system, to see whether it should be continued or brought to an end. Impoverished colleges who wanted the system to continue had to submit their accounts for our consideration. The richer bursars on our committee ruthlessly viva'd the supplicant bursars to see whether any income was being understated and how far current poverty was the result of inefficient management or injudicious investment. In fact it was far more likely that it was the rich colleges who were operating ingenious devices to minimise their taxable income; but beggars could not be quizzers.

In the end even the hardest-nosed members of our committee accepted that there was a case for another round of taxation, particularly to cushion recent government cuts in grant-in-aid that were being passed on by the university to the colleges in the shape of reduced funding for joint appointments. The tax rates our committee proposed, however, were blocked by two of the wealthy colleges, Queen's and Magdalen. In theory council could fix the rate of taxation without colleges' consent, but its proposals might well be defeated in congregation if the objecting colleges wheeled out their members to vote against them. Even if the proposals were carried, the objecting colleges might go to law against the university; the outcome was uncertain but the costs would be substantial. So our committee capitulated and accepted a reduction in the proposed rate. It was a classic example of Oxford's vulnerability, in the absence of effective mechanisms to co-ordinate college activities, to obstruction by maverick institutions.

Some years earlier a commission presided over by Lord Franks had attempted to remedy this. Instead of an anarchical collection of equipollent self-governing corporations, incapable of collective action if even a single college opposes, Franks wished to set up a senate of colleges which could bind each of its members by majority vote. This was too much for Oxford conservatives, and the conference of colleges which was set up in its place had no power to bind its members. The conference was little more than a talking shop, to which each college would send its head, plus one other fellow (commonly a bursar) to make sure that the head did not speak out of turn.

As Master of Balliol I was a regular attender at the Conference, was soon elected to its standing committee, and in due course became chairman. I discovered that the one effective organ of the conference was a small committee of bursars, who were entrusted with the annual negotiation of the level of college fees. The bursars were a good match for the officials in the Department of Education and regularly secured fee increases which at least kept pace with inflation.

Hebdomadal Council and Libraries Board

In 1980 I was elected to hebdomadal council, an elected body of some two dozen members presided over by the Vice-Chancellor which, in the 1980s met weekly in term time and at least once in each vacation. Members, wearing their black gowns, met on Monday afternoons around a ring of glossy tables in a featureless room in Wellington Square. Proceedings always began with prayers: "Prevent us, O Lord, in all our doings" the VC would intone. When I joined council I was told, and for a while believed, that if you had not arrived in time for prayers you were not allowed to vote.

The agendas for the Monday meetings were delivered by messenger to members' colleges on Friday evenings. A heavy envelope which might contain up to a hundred pages of paper would thud through the letter box, heavily stamped in red "Hebdomadal Council: Urgent". In fact much of the business of council was largely formal. Important matters reached it only after extensive discussion by lower bodies such as the University Chest or the Curators of libraries, museums, and other institutions, and it was rare for council to reach a decision different from the one recommended. But the business, during the years I attended council, was conducted soberly and efficiently. Roy Jenkins, who once attended council as Chancellor, told me that members' mastery of briefs, and level of discussion, compared favourably with many a cabinet meeting he had attended in 10 Downing Street.

Hebdomadal council, however, was not a university cabinet, because its members did not, as such, have departmental responsibilities. However, individual members might be appointed to chair the committees which oversaw the activities of the different departments and institutions of the university, and would thus become the university analogue of a cabinet minister. Thus, I became chair of the Libraries Board, with responsibility for the university library system.

There were altogether nearly a hundred university libraries to be funded. (The individual college libraries, many of which had important historic collections, were not under our jurisdiction.) However, eighty per cent of our budget was handed on to the Curators of the Bodleian Library, who had responsibility not only for the historic buildings in the centre of the university and the hideous New Bodleian across the Broad, but also for the Radcliffe Camera, the Radcliffe Science Library, the Rhodes House Library, the Law Library and a number of Oriental libraries.

The constitutional relationship between the Libraries Board and the Curators of the Bodleian was bizarre. As chair of the Board I reported ultimately to the Vice-Chancellor; but it was the Vice-Chancellor who chaired the Curators, whose budget was determined by my Boards. This Alice-in-Wonderland relationship reflected the main problem of the library system, which was the relationship between Bodley and the other libraries. Any attempt to achieve co-ordination between them all was seen by the smaller libraries as a Bodley take-over, and by Bodley as a threat to its unique international status. Some years later I was asked to chair a committee to rationalise this state of affairs, and there is now much greater co-operation between the different libraries.

Oxford spent a greater proportion of its income on libraries than any other university in the UK: this served it well when league tables were drawn up, but our board was constantly told of the need to reduce library expenditure, by such measures as minimising the duplication of purchases, amalgamating smaller collections, and achieving greater cooperation between different institutions.

One of our main responsibilities was arranging for the creation of a university-wide computerised catalogue of Oxford's holdings. The Bodleian was already far advanced in computerising its own catalogue, but the penalty of being ahead of the field in a technological age is that one is left with antiquated software. In order to automate a new unified catalogue, we spent much time listening to presentations by different firms, and pilot schemes were tried out in three faculty libraries. After much discussion and expert advice, we backed a loser (Dobis-Libis) and turned down the system which soon became standard world-wide (OCLC). Initially, a number of colleges were unwilling to join the unified catalogue: they did not wish their holdings to be known to non-members of their colleges.

Committees of council

Another committee of council of which I was for some years a member, though never chair, was the staff committee. This acted as the management side in negotiations with representatives of the University's employees. It dealt with four different unions, one for the janitorial staff, one for the technicians, one for the clerical and library staff, and one—the Association of University Teachers—for academic and academic-related staff. Our main task was to hold the ring between the professors in the large scientific departments ("the science barons") and the research workers and technicians employed by them. Individual members of the committees, in panels of two or three, spent much time adjudicating disputes about grading or applying grievance procedures.

While nationally the AUT was a militant though ineffective union, its local branch was mild and conservative. Negotiations between the University and the AUT had an air of farce, as both sides of the table consisted largely of dons who were working side by side in other contexts. More importantly, most of the union's members were college fellows who were largely responsible, in their governing bodies, for fixing their own salaries and terms of employment, oblivious of any worry about conflicts of interest.

At one time I was in the particularly Gilbertian position of being a member of the management team and also chairman of the local union branch. I cannot recall having many duties as a trades unionist: the oddest of them was to form part of a small university delegation in 1981 to wait on the Queen at Buckingham Palace to present a Loyal Address in congratulation on the engagement of the Prince of Wales to Lady Diana Spencer.

Having served as Master of Balliol for eleven years I resigned, as I had said I would do when I was first elected. I became instead Warden of Rhodes House, and secretary of the Rhodes Trust, which was my employer for the next ten years. I did not sever all links with the collegiate university. St John's College offered me a non-stipendiary professorial fellowship, and I continued for a while to sit on hebdomadal council. I was also for some years a Pro-Vice-Chancellor, at that time a purely ceremonial office which involved no more than presiding, in place of the Vice-Chancellor, at university sermons, inaugural lectures, and degree ceremonies. Later, Pro-Vice-Chancellors might find themselves chairing electoral committees for professorships, and by the end of the millennium there was a quorum of full-time working pro-vice-chancellors with ministerial portfolios.

A professorial fellow stands in a very different relation to his college from a tutorial fellow. Though a member of governing body, and entitled to the pleasures of college hospitality, he is unlikely to hold any college office or to have any great influence on college policy. I was welcomed warmly and generously to St John's, and having ample premises at Rhodes House I needed to make no claim on college accommodation or facilities. Not all professors in other colleges were as comfortable as I was, as I knew from experience at Balliol which in those days had something of a reputation for meanness towards its professors. Colleges were, in fact, ambivalent in their attitude to professorships. When a new chair was created, there would be keen bidding to have it attached to one's own college; but once the professor was installed he might find his presence, and demand on facilities, regarded as more of a burden than a benefit.

Apart from the University Press, which I will discuss in a later chapter, my only new experience of working within the university during my Rhodes years was serving on committees to recognize distinction. These committees were set up in response to government pressure to introduce performance pay. Individuals would apply for titular promotion in the university hierarchy, or to receive a supplement of salary, on the basis of their research record. Our committee would distribute titles and bonuses on the basis of expert assessment from outside the university. It was a fascinating but disagreeable job. I fear that the pain given to unsuccessful applicants was far greater than the pleasure given to successful ones, and I doubt whether the whole scheme made anyone work a jot harder in their chosen field of research, though it may have led some to publish more frequently, and perhaps kept them at Oxford when they were tempted to leave.

My final involvement with Oxford's university affairs came at the end of the millennium when, after retiring from Rhodes House, I was made president of the university's development campaign. I did not enjoy this job, I was not good at it, and I was glad when it was over. But it gave me a clear picture of the strains of a collegiate university. Many colleges, being wealthier than the central university, could tempt development staff away, once we had trained them, by offering them higher salaries to work in their own development offices. College fund-raising was quite separate and independent of university fund-raising, and we who were seeking money for the university were, by protocol, forbidden to solicit any Oxford graduate without the permission of his or her college. Alumni, the rule was, were alumni not of Oxford University, but of St Jude's College.

Chapter 3

Oxford from Next Door

Life in Rhodes House offers a privileged view of Oxford from outside. A Warden of Rhodes House has four main tasks. As Secretary of the Rhodes Trust he is chief (and sole) executive officer of a charitable foundation whose assets, at the turn of the century, approached £200m. As international secretary of the Rhodes scholarship scheme, he has to keep in touch with national secretaries who in twenty countries organise locally the selection of scholars. Once the scholars are selected it is his task to place them in colleges and on courses in Oxford, and to provide their funding, monitor their performance and offer back-up pastoral care during their time on stipend. Finally he is responsible for the upkeep and management of Rhodes House itself, which contains part of the Bodleian library and also a set of monumental rooms often used for academic and charitable purposes.

Though, as Warden, I was no longer an employee of the university, each of these tasks gave me an opportunity to observe it from close and novel viewpoints.

The Trust was governed by eight Trustees, by tradition four from Oxford and four from London. The London Trustees in my time included Lord Ashburton, Lord Armstrong of Ilminster, Lord Sainsbury of Preston Candover, and the Conservative cabinet minister William Waldegrave. As Warden I was fortunate to be able to draw on the financial and political expertise thus represented; without it, my task would have been impossible. Unlike the Oxford colleges in those years, the Trust was a charity registered with the charity commissioners, obliged to present accounts in accordance with the commissioners' statements of recommended practice. I was immediately struck by the amount of information these accounts contained, by comparison with the very guarded annual statements I had been accustomed to seeing from the colleges.

Because the Rhodes accounts were presented in a standardised form it was possible to compare our performance with that of other similar charities: I discovered that in the national league table of charities dependent on endowment, our assets placed us up there around the twentieth place, just behind Guide Dogs for the Blind. At Balliol I had not had any idea how our performance compared even with that of our neighbour Trinity, since college accounts then contained only statements of investment income, without a balance sheet to reveal the endowment capital.

The main charge on the Trust was of course the maintenance of the Rhodes scholars, but there was usually a substantial annual surplus to disburse on charitable purposes. Apart from educational causes in South Africa, the principal beneficiaries of the Trust in the nineteen nineties were the colleges and the university of Oxford. In 1988 the Trustees had provided the administration expenses to set up Campaign for Oxford, the central university's major capital appeal. Over the next five years they contributed a further two and a half million for a variety of purposes, from the endowment of posts in archaeology and management to the provision of child care and an all-weather running track. In later years donations continued at a roughly similar level, but more often to colleges than to the central university.

A jilted benefactor

The Rhodes Trustees were among Oxford's most generous and flexible of funders, but as their representative I became aware that the university does not always treat its benefactors with the degree of consideration they might expect. This was strikingly illustrated when the Trust offered to help out with one of Oxford's long-standing problems, namely the status of academic staff who lack college fellowships.

Rhodes House stands on a road lined with university laboratories. The professors and senior academic staff of the science departments are, like their colleagues in arts subjects, fellows of colleges. Towards the end of the twentieth century, however, many of the academics in the laboratories were employed on fixed-term contracts supported by research grants, which did not carry entitlement to fellowships. Though they were no less academically competent than their non-scientific colleagues, they belonged to no senior common room and depended for social facilities on a meagre club called Halifax House. Already by 1991 there were 1,600 research staff on outside grants and contracts, and the low level of provision for them was regarded by many in the university as a scandal.

The Trustees in 1992 offered to hand over a significant part of Rhodes House to provide a large dining room and two ample common rooms for university staff from the science area. They were also willing to build a new wing to provide twenty bedrooms for academic visitors to the university. The offer was welcomed by the university. A number of architects presented plans for the expansion of Rhodes House, and the Trustees chose an elegant design by Robert Adam. The scheme, which was expected to cost about two and three quarter million pounds, was given planning approval, and the trustees appointed project managers and structural, electrical, and mechanical engineers. It was hoped that the building could be completed in 1995, and would then take over on a more adequate scale the functions of Halifax House, offering college-style accommodation in the science area.

Then, for reasons that were not explained to the Trustees for two years, the university lost interest in the project. The first intimation I had of this was when the kitchen of the new Rhodes House was being designed. I invited the chef of Halifax House to take part in the discussion, since if all went according to plan he would be moving there with his staff in a couple of years. "Oh, haven't you heard?" he said "It's all off".

It was only in 1996 that the university publicly announced the reason. Mr Wafic Said had offered a generous benefaction to build a school of business studies on a green field site on Mansfield Road. This would displace a club for the university's technical staff, and the senior university authorities had decided that rather than accept Rhodes House as a home for the academic staff, they would prefer a purpose-built social facility for academics, technicians, and graduate students.

Ironically, the project for a business school on Mansfield Road came to nothing. It transpired that the offer of the site contravened a pledge, made when the land was acquired from Merton thirty years earlier, that the land would remain green in perpetuity. When the matter came before congregation it voted, quite rightly, against the assignment of the site to the business school.

By now Mr Said, as well as the Rhodes Trust, had good reason to feel aggrieved. But both benefactors swallowed whatever outrage they may have felt, and continued their philanthropy to the university. A new site was found for the Said School near the railway station, and the Rhodes Trustees transferred their savings to a different project, the Rothermere American Institute. Rhodes House remained unaltered, and a new university club was built on the site of the old technicians' club on Mansfield Rd.

The placement of Rhodes scholars

For the Warden of Rhodes House, every December fat packets arrive from four continents. These contain the documentation of the scholars-elect who have been chosen by the committees in their home countries. Selection as a Rhodes Scholar does not guarantee a place in Oxford University or any of its colleges, and it is the Warden's task, on the basis of this documentation, to seek admission on behalf of the scholars.

In my time the candidates were all graduates of an overseas university, but some of them, especially from the United States, wished to read for a second B.A. Application on behalf of these was made to individual colleges, since the colleges controlled undergraduate admission. For those who wished to read for master's degrees or to pursue a doctorate, application was made to the university's graduate studies office, which passed the documentation to the relevant faculty committee. These dossiers only went on to colleges after the candidate had secured admission from the faculty.

Ten years' experience of this job made me aware of the immense complexity of Oxford's admissions procedures. For BA applicants an individual college might require in the way of documentation something slightly different from its next door neighbour. Applications for a particular degree might be welcome at college A, but be turned down by college B. If a scholar-elect was rejected by his college of first choice, I might have to apply to three or four other colleges to obtain admission, so that a scholar elected in December might be still without a place in June. Mastering the requirements of particular colleges was quite a difficult task for someone who had spent much of his life in Oxford: it might well seem insurmountable to schoolboys and schoolgirls from families and schools with no previous Oxbridge experience.

Graduate admissions were simpler, since they passed through a single office. But behind that gateway the faculties differed greatly in the speed and efficiency with which they dealt with applications. A particularly irritating practice of some faculties was called "waiting for the gathered field". The idea was not to admit any student in advance of the latest possible date for application. This meant, again, that an applicant might be kept waiting from January to June without a decision on his application. The aim of this tactic was to ensure that no place should be given away to an early applicant which might prevent its award to a later, academically superior, candidate. But it was a self-defeating policy, since some of the most highly qualified applicants got tired of waiting, and accepted an offer from some other university, even though Oxford was their first choice. Rhodes scholars, since their funding was tied to Oxford, did not have this possibility, and had no option but to suffer the months of suspense.

Once the scholars had been admitted to colleges and faculties, I had the responsibility of providing the stipends for their maintenance and paying the university and college fees. Once again, the multiplicity of colleges increased enormously the workload of our office — as it must have done for local authority offices throughout the country during the years when they had responsibility for fees. Each college would have a slightly different method and schedule for invoicing, and each invoice had to be carefully checked.

Pastoral care and academic progress

But while my time at Rhodes House made me aware of the bureaucratic disadvantages of the college system, it also put me in a unique position to appreciate its pastoral merits. Rhodes Scholars were often dissatisfied with the university course to which they had been admitted, and in some years more than a quarter of them would apply for my permission to change course. But it was extremely rare for scholars to ask to change their college. Within the very first term scholars seemed to acquire a special loyalty to the college of which they were a member — and this was true even of those who had been rejected by their colleges of choice. This loyalty, moreover, lasted throughout life: scholars returning to Oxford after years in business or professions abroad made contact with their old colleges and their staff. Bill Clinton, returning as President of the US, took pains to visit not only his old tutor but also the head porter: his nostalgic affection was typical of many less well-known Rhodes scholars.

For the first fifty years of its existence Rhodes House served as a pastoral centre for scholars in trouble. The warden and his wife would take in sick and injured scholars, and provide comfortable accommodation during convalescence. In our time this was no longer so necessary. College sick bays had become much more attractive environments, and I was regularly impressed by the medical care the colleges provided. We did sometime accommodate convalescents, but the improvement in air fare meant that convalescents would often prefer us to pay to fly them to their home, rather than take them into ours. Sometimes it would be their parents whom we accommodated while the patients themselves convalesced in college. Altogether our experience of the care provided by colleges was very positive. Our back-up role was rarely called upon—but sometimes it was needed in an intercollegiate context e.g. to sort out an allegation of harassment made by a scholar in one college against a scholar in another.

From 1989–93 I was President of the British Academy, which is to the humanities and social sciences what the Royal Society is to the sciences. At that period the Department of Education and Science had delegated to the Academy the provision of graduate scholarships to British students. The government was concerned about the low rate of completion of doctorates: many who had held scholarships had still not completed their theses seven years after coming on stipend. We at the Academy were told to improve matters under pain of a reduction in the funds available. Some of my colleagues were incensed about this government intervention, but it seemed to me to reflect a legitimate concern about whether taxpayers' money was being used for the purposes for which it was intended. The DES was not in fact imposing new rules for graduates: it only wanted us to urge universities to enforce their own rules on completion rates.

Oxford was one of the universities with the largest number of humanities graduates, and the Academy discovered that it did not do particularly well in the league table for completion of dissertations. As President I had occasion to write letters to the heads of a number of colleges, asking them to explain the poor rates of their students. Altogether, both at the Academy and at Rhodes House, as well as in my years at Balliol, I formed the impression that the supervision of graduates was one of the weakest points of the Oxford system.

Graduate students, as I came to realise, are the least well favoured members of the Oxford community. The supervision of postgraduates was regarded and remunerated as an extra, spare-time, activity for dons who saw themselves as primarily undergraduate teachers. Oxford was for a long time unusual in that a graduate student could obtain a research degree by thesis alone. A student at one of the better US graduate schools would not be awarded a doctorate without attending a number of specialised courses and passing a number of comprehensive examinations. Again, a typical graduate student in the US is assigned a committee of several members to guide in the writing of a dissertation. In Oxford only a single supervisor is assigned, and if that supervisor was lazy or incompetent a student could lead a very lonely and frustrating life.

A number of internal Oxford reports between 1966 and the present day have emphasized the need for the university to pay greater attention to its graduate students. In many subjects it is now the common practice for a doctoral dissertation to be preceded by a taught Master's course, which brings graduate students together and reduces their isolation. Since 1991 doctoral candidates have to spend a preparatory year as a probationary research student. These are welcome improvements, but it is difficult to be confident that all the grievances of graduate students have been redressed.

Oxford University Press

In my last years at Balliol and my first years at Rhodes House I was a delegate of Oxford University Press. This gave me an opportunity to see the university at its most business-like. The Press is the publishing arm of the university and is one of the most important vehicles by which it carries out its educational mission. There are people in many parts of the world who know nothing of Oxford except its Press, and OUP's dictionary makers have brought the university as much prestige as any of its faculties.

The delegates form the committee which is responsible to the University for the running of the Press. In my day there were sixteen of us, each chosen for expertise in a particular subject; we met, gowned, under the chairmanship of the Vice-Chancellor on alternate Tuesday mornings in the Clarendon Building, the Press's original home. Our task was to approve a list of academic titles to go to contract. The actual work of commissioning, drawing up contracts, copy-editing, book production and marketing was of course the responsibility of professional publishers. But each subject editor worked closely with the relevant delegate, who saw all significant correspondence between editor, author, and referees. When a proposal was ripe for contract a one-page summary of the title, with projected print-run and investment required, was presented by the delegate to his colleagues for approval. If referees were ambiguously in favour, and editor and delegate agreed on the merits of a book, it went through on the nod, and it was possible in a two-hour meeting to deal with sixty books or more. But at each meeting there would be one or two controversial proposals that needed lengthy discussion.

More significant than the delegacy itself is its finance committee. This is in effect the board of directors of a multi-million pound business with branches it many countries — the Press's American branch is bigger in its own right than any academic publisher in the US. Finance committee had a very different ethos from the delegates meeting: the Vice-Chancellor did not preside, no gowns were worn, and meetings were held not in the antique splendour of the Clarendon building but in a glossy office in the press's new premises in Walton St. I was one of six delegates who sat on the committee. Alongside two outside members with business experience (Tim Rix and Martin Jacomb) we were in effect the non-executive members of the board, while the executive directors were the professional publishers who headed the different divisions of the Press. Unlike the full delegates meeting we concentrated not so much on academic monographs but on other more profitable areas: schools educational publishing, English as a foreign language, and reference and general books.

The governance arrangements were — as in the case of libraries, mentioned in the previous chapter — anomalous. The delegacy, which was in effect merely an academic advisory board, was in theory sovereign over the finance committee, which for practical purposes was the board of the company. Despite this, the system worked well, and the Press has maintained high academic standards while becoming ever more profitable. Each year since the 1980s it has produced healthy annual surpluses which can be used to assist the university — unlike most university presses in the US which are subsidized by their parent bodies. In addition to supporting the university, OUP has funded research projects on a substantial scale, such as the massive Oxford Dictionary of National Biography in sixty volumes, which was produced on time, and within budget, in 2005.

I left the Press when, in 1993 I was appointed by the Secretary of State for National Heritage to be chairman of the board of the British Library. I could foresee that this new post could give rise to conflicts of interest with great publishing firms. The British Library has the right to acquire a free copy of every book published in the UK and this right of legal deposit is regarded by some publishers as burdensome.

Chancellor Jenkins

During my years at Rhodes House I became friendly with Roy Jenkins, then Chancellor of the University, and we discussed Oxford matters together over many a pub lunch. Roy was concerned at the way in which diminished state funding for the universities went hand in hand with increasing government interference in their management.

To remedy the first problem, he took advantage of his friendship with Tony Blair to press on his attention the threat that continued underfunding presented to the academic prestige of Britain's great universities. The University of Salamanca, he once reminded him, used to be one of the most celebrated universities of the world. Unless urgent remedies were applied to the financial plight of universities, Oxford, like Salamanca, might altogether fade from global consciousness.

With regard to the second problem, Roy became convinced that only independence from government funding and control would enable universities like Oxford and Cambridge to remain in the same class as the Ivy League universities in the US. He was unwilling to express this opinion publicly since it was not the policy of the university, but he once said to me that he was willing to devote the rest of his life to help bring it about.

I was uncertain about the practicality of privatising Oxbridge, but I was sufficiently impressed by Roy's concern to devise a plan whereby the financial possibilities might be explored. I asked a friend in the US who chaired a prestigious foundation whether his board would be willing to fund a comparative study of the funding of British and American higher education — a study to be carried out by some independent think-tank, such as the Brookings Institute. His reaction was favourable, so the next step was to decide which institution or institutions should apply to the foundation for funding for the study. An application by either of the Oxbridge universities would seem too self-serving, as they were the only two institutions in the UK whose endowments were large enough to make the prospect of privatisation remotely realistic. So who should take on the application?

I thought I had hit on the ideal solution. The Royal Society and the British Academy were not universities in receipt of public funding, yet they had a clear interest in maintaining the standards of advanced teaching and research in the UK. On the margins of a conference in Philadelphia in 2001 I was able to bring around a table the presidents of the two institutions with my foundation chairman. All agreed to co-operate, and I was jubilant.

Not for long, however. When the two Presidents returned home they were disowned by their councils. There was a danger, it was felt, that the government would be offended by the commission of such a study, and so no further step should be taken. In fact, I had been assured informally that such a study would not be unwelcome in 10 Downing St, though it might not be similarly well received by David Blunkett in the Department of Education.

I am sad that no impartial, expert, assessment of the finances of privatisation has been undertaken. Later in the book we offer our own partisan and amateur discussion of the topic.

Chapter 4

A History of Reforms

In recent debates about Oxford governance it was often asserted by those who opposed reform that a system that has served the university well for eight hundred years ought not to be rashly altered. In fact Oxford's current machinery of government is a piecemeal creation of the nineteenth and twentieth centuries.

In 1800 there was in Oxford little that resembled either the colleges or the university of the present day. The colleges existed, indeed, as closed corporations variously endowed; but there was nothing like the tutorial system that is nowadays regarded as the colleges' most valuable contribution to education. Four imposing buildings constituted the visible presence of the university: the Church of St Mary in the High Street, the Sheldonian theatre for grand ceremonials, the Bodleian library for the voluntary pursuit of learning, and the Clarendon Building to house the University Press.

The sovereign body of the university was convocation, the gathering of all Oxford MAs from across the nation. But the university's executive (the hebdomadal board) was simply the assembly of the heads of the colleges, one of whom took his turn to preside for a couple of years as Vice-Chancellor, afforced by two disciplinary officers, the Proctors, elected year by year by a different college in accordance with a rota. It was, indeed, the university that conferred the degrees of BA and MA and doctorates in certain subjects; but it did not prescribe any serious examinations as a condition of these distinctions. There were a number of professorships funded by the university, with lecturing duties, but the stipends were modest, and many professors were non-resident.

It was the reform of the examination system that was the first step towards the modern university. Statutes of 1800 and 1807 set up classified honour schools in literae humaniores (classics) and in science and mathematics. Colleges appointed tutors to give lectures on the texts set for the examination, but one-on-one tutorial teaching was in fact carried out by privately hired "coaches" outside the college system. There were college tutors who wished to widen their responsibilities: John Henry Newman and some of his Oriel colleagues thought that a tutor should have pastoral as well as lecturing functions. But this proposal was too entwined with the theological agenda of the Oxford movement to find favour with the authorities, and the Oriel tutors had to resign. In a university which was confined to members of the Church of England, many college fellows were content to see their fellowships as a congenial bachelor start to a clerical career which would lead on to a cure of souls in a college living permitting matrimony.

Others at the opposite pole from Newman likewise called for an expansion of tutorial duties. A critic from Edinburgh wrote in 1850 "The possession of a fellowship implies the right to receive so much money for doing nothing". A duty should be placed on fellows of imparting public instruction, he said, and fellows should be allowed to marry, so that they had no inducement to leave the university. 557 fellowships in the colleges could be transformed into some 200 professorships to give instruction in progressive sciences.

The first Royal Commissions

Complaints and cries for reform grew into a national chorus which led, in 1850, to the appointment of a Royal Commission to inquire into the discipline, studies, and revenues of both Oxford and Cambridge. From the outset the commission was bitterly opposed at Oxford. The hebdomadal board and most current fellows of colleges denied its legitimacy and refused to offer evidence or provide information. Cambridge was little more enthusiastic. G.E. Corrie, Master of Jesus College there was asked by the Commission what he felt were the greatest needs of the university. He responded: "The present chief want of the University is exemption from the disturbing power of Royal or Parliamentary Commissions". [1]

The members of the commission and those who submitted evidence were mainly liberals who had long expressed dissatisfaction with the closed and clerical nature of the collegiate universities. The commission's recommendations for Oxford, when they were published in a Blue Book in 1852, were radical. Hebdomadal board was to be abolished, and the government of the university was to be in the hands of a congregation of around a hundred, in which professors would form a majority. Under the professors there would be a

---

[1]   Robert Kenny, *This College Studded Marsh*, 1989

tier of university lecturers specialising in different disciplines. College tutors would form the lowest level of the academic hierarchy, taking over the role of the private coaches. It was hoped that, after some years as tutors, fellows might aspire to become lecturers or professors, rather than to pursue a clerical career, and if so they should be allowed to marry. The professors would pursue research and control examinations, and they would appoint the lecturers who, with the college tutors, would bear the brunt of the teaching. Their chairs would be attached to colleges, which would, by suppressing existing fellowships, provide the endowments to pay them handsome salaries.

The commissioners' recommendations went far beyond anything hitherto proposed or subsequently enacted. They were too much for the Chancellor of the university, the Duke of Wellington, who took the Blue Book and a pencil to bed with him, muttering "I'll never get through it", and died in his sleep that same night. They were too much not only for the hebdomadal board, but also for the college tutors who, stung by the proposal to make them academic helots of the professors, formed a sixty-strong Tutors Association to bring forward alternative proposals. Finally, they were too much for the government which, in the person of the university's MP, William Ewart Gladstone, steered the eventual Oxford University Act through Parliament in 1854.

The Act made no mention of an academic pyramid surmounted by a professoriate. It did, however, make significant changes in the government of the university. The convocation of all MAs, which had been dominated by country clergy, remained in theory supreme, but the effective sovereign role passed to a new (or rather, revived) assembly called congregation, to consist only of resident MAs. The Act abolished the old hebdomadal board of heads of houses and replaced it by an elected hebdomadal council. These were lasting changes: congregation underwent a substantial reform early in the twentieth century so that it contained only residents working for the university, rather than all MAs who happened to live in Oxford, but in its modified form it remains to this day the sovereign body of the university. Hebdomadal council remained the executive of the university until the twenty-first century.

The colleges got off much more lightly. Instead of the massive spoliation proposed by the Commission, the Act merely gave colleges the power to remodel their statutes (then dating from the 1630s) in consultation with a new group of executive commissioners, who were all loyal college men. The only provision of the Act that had an immediate effect on colleges was the permission it gave for non-Anglicans to matriculate and take a BA — a reform inserted at a late stage of the legislative process on the initiative of a unitarian MP. But even this reform was muted, since the colleges continued to reserve scholarships and fellowships to members of the Church of England, until all religious tests were abolished by act of parliament in 1871. The obligation of celibacy remained, and college endowments remained untouched.

The effect of the Act of 1854 and of the subsequent reforms of college statutes was to enhance the influence of college tutors. They formed the largest group in the new congregation, which had the power to elect the members of the new council (six heads, six professors, and six other members of convocation). Tutors began to take over, voluntarily, the coaching duties that the Commissioners wished to impose on them. But tutors remained a minority in the colleges, with most fellowships still being held as sinecures — lifelong sinecures, if the fellow was willing to forego marriage.

Unsurprisingly, reformers were deeply disappointed at the outcome of this first Royal Commission. In the 1870s two linked Commissions bit more deeply into Oxford's traditional fabric. The Cleveland Commission of 1871 had as its remit merely to collect financial information about Oxbridge and its colleges, but the figures that it published heightened the clamour for reform, since they showed how little of Oxford's vast endowment was actually used for educational purposes. Of the £414k income derived from land £48k went to the university and £366k to the colleges, where most of the money went to support the heads and fellows, only £26k going for scholarships. The tuition funds, which were financed by fees, and which provided the stipends of tutors and lecturers, were more or less in balance overall. A striking figure was that in 1871 while only £7k was paid to university professors, £9k was spent in augmenting the salaries of ex-fellows in college livings

Pressure for further government intervention came this time from Oxford itself, appropriately enough from Dean Liddell of Christ Church, the father of Alice of Wonderland. At his request Disraeli's government set up a new royal commission in 1877 by an Act which declared it "expedient that provision be made for enabling or requiring the Colleges in each university to contribute more largely out of their revenues to University purposes". The commissioners were entitled to write completely new statutes for the colleges, with or without college consent.

The commissioners, chaired by Lord Selborne, failed in fact to make any significant impact on the poverty of the university in relation to the colleges. A new Common University Fund was set up to fund professorships and readerships and laboratories. It was to be funded by a levy on colleges, with a basic rate of 2% on annual endowment income, rising to 16% for the richest, Magdalen and Christ Church. The tax, however, was phased in very gently, and the absolute sums that were handed over to the university proved much smaller than expected, because of the agricultural depression that reduced college incomes in the last decades of the century. By 1913 college payments to the university amounted to only 16 per cent of its revenue.

The more lasting effect of the 1877 commission was on the internal structure of the colleges. A new class of "official fellowships" was created, for tutors and other college officers, which permitted marriage; the tenure of non-official fellowships was now limited to seven years. Gradually, in most colleges, the number of these "prize-fellowships" diminished, until by 1914 only All Souls retained a significant number. Colleges were empowered, but not forced, to give fellowships to university professors and readers, and a new class of research fellows was created. Colleges were allowed to set their expenses on research fellowships against the sums due to the university under the new taxation scheme, and the richer colleges made great use of this loophole.

Finally, the commissioners set up faculty boards to oversee the examination system and to co-ordinate (by voluntary methods) a university-wide system of lecturing, with a view to reducing wasteful duplication of bread-and-butter college lectures and encouraging lectures on a greater variety of topics. Initially there were four faculty boards, theology, law, natural science, and arts. These boards later split, as other honour schools were added to the traditional ones, and in 1910 all faculty boards were brought under a General Board, which continued in existence until the 21st century.

Women and science

The most significant change in Oxford in the late years of the nineteenth century was the admission of women to the university. In 1879 two new Halls, Somerville and Lady Margaret were opened. However, it was not until 1920 that women were allowed to matriculate and take degrees, and an influential group of dons successfully resisted reform of any kind, especially reform in the spirit of the 1887 commission. The non-placet society was founded "to criticize modern innovations". It consisted not of old dons, but of young ones, who resented their own fellowships being restricted to seven years while their seniors could now marry and hold on to their tutorships for life. It was particularly opposed to any expansion of scientific research in the university: it made its organ the recently founded Oxford Magazine.

An Exeter don, L.R. Farnell, founded a group to counteract the Non-placets. "Its aim was mainly to maintain and develop the character of the University as a home of learning and science and for this purpose to place the interests of the University as a whole above those of the separate colleges". When, early in the twentieth century, Farnell attempted as Vice-Chancellor to put some of his reforming ideas into practice, he received a box of contaminated chocolates. At first interpreted as a murder attempt, the chocolates were found on examination to contain only toothpaste.

It took a world war to give science its proper place at Oxford. In a war in which high explosives and poison gas were important determinants of victory, the need for scientifically trained manpower soon made itself obvious. In 1915, as the history of the university puts it "the chemists were the heroes of the hour". Though the Oxford colleges offered up arts graduates in their thousands to serve in the war — one in five of whom were killed — the university was producing only one hundred finalists a year in science subjects. Lloyd George set up a committee on science education in Britain, which in 1918 recommended that Greek should no longer be compulsory for entrance to Oxford.

The Minister for Education, H.A.L. Fisher, decided that Oxford had no hope of keeping up with developments in applied science without help from the state. The first government grants were made in 1919. Further subvention, Oxford was told, would depend on the government being assured that the university was well governed and managed, and for this purpose he proposed yet another Royal Commission. Council and congregation agreed, though the Oxford Magazine inquired indignantly whether "we" were to "sacrifice our independence" to save "ourselves the trouble of finding elsewhere the necessary funds for the equipment of our laboratories" [2]

---

[2]   John Prest, in HUO, VIII, 30

The commission was headed by the former Prime Minister, Herbert Asquith, a Balliol classics don of 1874 and from the colleges' point of view a safe pair of hands. Reformers suggested to the Commission that the university should supervise college finances and appropriate any surplus income. This proposal was firmly rejected. "Such a change would impair the vigour of college life and hamper educational development.... The strength of the two universities is very largely due to the existence of a number of independent colleges acting in wholesome competition with one another, and we are convinced that it would be a grave mistake to subject them to final control by the Universities and to deprive them of the power of initiating new policy."[3]

Though the Asquith commission did give the collegiate university a tilt in the direction of science it did so in the gentlest possible manner. It would indeed have been difficult to argue at that moment that it was in the interests of science that the university should be strengthened at the expense of the colleges, because the Professor of Chemistry from 1872 to 1912 had carried out no research, while half a dozen colleges had opened laboratories at their own initiative.

The commission struck a balance between university and college interests by insisting that all professors must be found fellowships in colleges, and all college tutors must receive appointment as a university lecturer. This set the general pattern of academic employment for most of the rest of the century. As for the advancement of science — the number of finalists was doubled, but the influx of scientists was barely noticeable behind a further expansion of the arts.

These three great royal commissions all followed a similar pattern. Each was set up with a remit to make a radical change in the balance of power between colleges and university. Each initially favoured a substantial increase in university funding and authority. In each case the eventual outcome was a watered down system of reform, which left the colleges in possession of the greater part of the field. No further royal commissions have been set up. Such changes in the governance of Oxford as have since occurred have been the result either of internal pressure for reform or of government diktat without benefit of the stately consultation of a commission.

The great innovation of the post-war period was Oxford's acceptance (by a congregation vote of 126 votes to 88) of funding from the government. For half a century this was administered with the minimum of government interference. State funds were distributed at

[3]   Quoted by John Dunbabin, in HUO VIII, 642

arm's length by a University Grants Committee composed of academics, and the sums disbursed were comparatively modest. Oxford's first annual grant was £30k, and in 1937-8 it was still no more than £110k. At the same time Oxford was able to attract substantial funds from private philanthropists, its income from such sources gradually coming to surpass all other British universities. This was largely due to the motor manufacturer Lord Nuffield, whose benefactions to the university between the wars amounted to twice the amount received from the Treasury. The New Bodleian library and Nuffield College remain as visible monuments of this era of philanthropy.[4]

Once again a world war stimulated government to generosity: in 1946 universities were invited to submit proposals for training scientists on the assumption that "the Treasury purse was open wide". By the early 1970s the UGC grant to Oxford represented two-thirds of its income. The extent of state aid altered the financial balance between the university and the colleges, and in 1952 the Vice-Chancellor drew the attention of the UGC to "the poverty of the colleges and the relative affluence of the university". The Common University Fund had survived the Asquith reforms, and despite regular complaints from bursars colleges continued until the 1960s to be taxed for the benefit of the university. Much of the take was spent on supporting CUF lecturerships. These were awarded to college tutors to give them time for research, in return for lectures that were open freely to the whole university. In the 1950s the UGC underwrote the extension of such a system of composite remuneration for all 286 intercollegiate lecturers. From then onwards, joint appointments became the norm. Surpluses in the CUF were use to make building loans to colleges, and from 1962 to make direct grants to the poorest societies.

Franks, North, and Hood

In 1963 a Prime Ministerial Committee headed by Lord Robbins produced a report which contained severe criticisms of Oxford. Robbins complained about the university's inability to reach rapid decisions, the opaqueness of its financial and administrative arrangements, its overpayment of staff, and the socially exclusive nature of its recruitment of students. If these shortcomings were not remedied, it was

---

[4]   HUO, X, 648

made clear, Oxford was in danger of being investigated by another Royal Commission.

To anyone looking back from the present day, Robbins' list of complaints is dishearteningly familiar. During the last forty years only one of the Robbins issues has been definitively laid to rest, and that is the problem of the overpayment of Oxford staff. The problem has been replaced by an equal and opposite one, the underpayment of Oxford staff.

But in 1964 Oxford made a serious effort to reform itself before any reforms were imposed from outside. An internal commission was set up under Lord Franks to report on Oxford's role in the United Kingdom's system of higher education, having regard to its position as both a national and an international university. Franks and his colleagues conscientiously collected evidence and proposed a number of reforms. Some were accepted and came into force. The shadowy powers of convocation were abolished, and only two were retained: the right to elect the Chancellor and the right to elect the professor of poetry. Other proposed reforms were voted down in congregation or rejected by the colleges. Nothing came of a proposal that the faculties should be grouped into five "super-faculties". A proposal that there should be a senate of colleges with the power to bind its members was emasculated, so that all that emerged was a conference of colleges which during its forty years' history has been little more than a forum for debate.

One of the most significant reforms, however, was accepted: a strengthening of the role of the Vice-Chancellor. Hitherto the Vice-Chancellorship had been held, for a period of two years, by the current head of Buggins college. Any longer period, it was felt, carried the danger that the VC might go native in Wellington Square, forgetting that he was first and foremost a head of house. Franks made three changes in the office. Henceforth a Vice-Chancellor was to be elected by congregation, on the nomination of an electoral college. Any member of congregation was eligible for election; and the successful candidate was to hold office for four years. It was now possible, for the first time, for someone who was not a head of a college to be elected Vice-Chancellor. Under the Franks statutes congregation exercised this option only once, and that not until Sir Richard Southwood, Professor of Zoology, was elected to take office in 1989.

Franks once told me that he had seen his role as being to redress, in favour of the university, a balance of power which had now, he felt, tilted too far towards the colleges. But one of his reforms had exactly the opposite effect. The common university fund was replaced by a college contributions fund which was designed not to assist the university, but to transfer funds from the richer colleges to the poorer colleges in order to bring their endowments up to a minimum level. Most dons continued to be called "CUF lecturers" but henceforth their income as lecturers was derived not from any college taxation, but entirely from university funds.

In the latter decades of the century a number of changes in the university's structure of governance came about by pressure rather than by design. When the nation decided that adolescents, on reaching the age of 18, became adults and were qualified to vote, the claim of the university to act in loco parentis to undergraduates was seen as an anachronism. In consequence of a report by the jurisprudent H.L.A. Hart the paternalistic disciplinary procedures of the proctors were modified, and junior members were allowed to speak in congregation and sit on university committees, including eventually hebdomadal council. But these reforms were not enough for the student generation that protested against the Vietnam war in the US and nearly brought down the government in France. Much of the time of senior members around 1970 was taken up listening to the grievances of junior members, preventing the disruption of academic business through sit-ins, and finding appropriate ways of disciplining student malefactors. The student troubles presented the outside world with the image of a chaotic university, which hampered the university authorities both in negotiating with government and in appealing to philanthropists.

In the early 70s it was widely agreed that it was desirable that some of the older colleges should open their gates to both sexes so as to balance the number of men and women in Oxford. With thirty or so colleges, it should have been possible to maximise choice for candidates by ending up with, say, twenty mixed colleges, five all-male colleges, and five all-female colleges. Hebdomadal council devised a scheme to provide for an orderly progression, whereby five male colleges at a time would take a quota of women. Vice-Chancellors were quite unable to enforce this scheme against the competitive ardour of the men's colleges all of whom, within a few years, rushed to admit women.

Many of the issues that had preoccupied the Franks commission were revisited in the 1990s by an another internal commission chaired by Sir Peter North (V-C from 1993–97). One of its recommendations was that a Vice-Chancellor should be appointed for five years, and then be re-eligible for a further two. It fell to North's successor, Sir Colin Lucas, to oversee the translation of the North recommendations into university legislation. Lucas later became the first Vice-Chancellor to hold office for seven years (1997–2004).

The North reforms were substantial. Hebdomadal council and the General Board were swept away: in their place, from 2000 onwards, the supreme executive body was a single Council, containing two external members. Four main committees of council were to deal with detailed business: Educational Policy and Standards, General Purposes, Personnel, and Policy and Resource Allocation (PRAC). The principal committees would be chaired by full-time Pro-Vice-Chancellors. In place of the General Board a new divisional structure was put in place, fulfilling after more than thirty years the Franks vision of five super-faculties. The new divisions were humanities, social sciences, medical sciences, plus two others which have since been amalgamated into a division of mathematical, physical, and life sciences. The new Pro-Vice-Chancellors and the heads of the divisions formed a substantial official presence on the new council. In 2002 these arrangements were codified in a complete new set of statutes, all previous university statutes being repealed. The Privy Council, in giving its approval to the new statutes, caused the number of external members of council to be doubled from two to four, and expressed the view that ideally there should be a lay majority.

Oxford's tardiness in reaching decisions had long been a standing complaint. It was hoped that the new governance structure would speed up decisions by devolving many issues from the centre to be dealt with at divisional level. It cannot be said that these hopes have been fulfilled. One of the main tasks of PRAC was to devise a resource allocation method (RAM), which would divide the available funds in an equitable way among the new divisions. This process went through many iterations. An admirably objective abstract formula would be devised, with one of its objects being to reward those activities that brought revenue into the university. It would then be discovered by the head of one or other division that this formula would lead to a sharp reduction in the funding of that division's faculties. Thereupon a new abstract formula would be devised, which would, incidentally, remedy this perceived underfunding. At this point a different head of division would detect that the new formula placed his or her division at a disadvantage, and a new cycle would begin.

The matter was further complicated when, in 2001, the Blair government decided to cease the payment of college fees and replace them with a block payment to the university. The colleges then had to be brought in to decide what was a fair allocation of the funds newly accruing to the university, and the RAM became a JRAM, a joint resource allocation mechanism.

It is difficult to decide whether the difficulties with the RAM reflected a structural defect in the new system of governance, or whether they were simply the kind of teething problems inevitable when new procedures are brought into operation. The decree of congregation approving the North statutes contained a clause calling for a review of the new governance structures after five years. But the system was not given such a period undisturbed.

Under the North reforms it was no longer necessary for a Vice-Chancellor-elect to be a member of congregation. The electors took advantage of this at the first possible opportunity, and when Lucas demitted office in 2004 he was succeeded by Dr John Hood, the Vice-Chancellor of Auckland University. Hood had been at Worcester College as a New Zealand Rhodes Scholar from 1976–8, when he obtained a BPhil in management studies. Most of his working life had been spent in the construction industry. Many people — with enthusiasm or apprehension according to taste — saw him as having been given a mandate to make Oxford more business-like. One of his first acts was to set up a working party to carry out a root-and-branch re-examination of the university's governance.

In March 2005 the working party produced a green paper for discussion. This was seen by many as far too dirigiste, and the Oxford Magazine published many articles of criticism. The working party took time to modify their proposals, and it was not until the Michaelmas term of 2006 that they were ready to bring forward a legislative proposal, a new version of Statute VI (Concerning Council).

The single council set up under the North reforms had found itself overburdened with work, and the new Statute revived bicameral government. The General Board was not restored: in its place an Academic Board was to be created, which would be larger than the old General Board because it would contain substantial college representation. As the working party's spokesman explained when introducing the measure in congregation, this body would have responsibility for setting and pursuing academic strategy for the collegiate university as whole. "As things stand" he said "a proposal for academic change has to move up two parallel ladders of committees: a university ladder, and a college ladder." It was, he said, extraordinary that no co-ordinating body of this kind had hitherto existed in Oxford.

The new council would no longer have responsibility for academic matters, but would control endowment, estates, budget, and external relations. It would be smaller than the current council, with only fifteen members, but the most significant difference would be that it would consist of an equal number of internal and external members, chaired, in the first instance, by the Chancellor, Lord (Chris) Patten. Like its predecessor, it would be subject to the overarching authority of congregation. The expansion of the lay membership was commended by the working party on both internal and external grounds: the university itself would benefit from the incorporation at its highest level of outside expertise and perspective, and its relations with public and private funders would be improved by the adoption of a mode of government favoured by HEFCE and the charity commissioners.

The proposal that lay members should form a majority on the university's council provoked uproar. It was denounced as the end of academic democracy in Oxford. The lay members would be philistines with no feeling for academic values. They would be catspaws of an overweening executive, keen to introduce into Oxford a form of managerialism already discredited in the business world. It was vain for defenders of the reform to point out that congregation would remain sovereign, that the outside members would be likely to be Oxford's own alumni, and that a council with a lay chair was more likely to hold the executive to account than one chaired by the Vice-Chancellor himself.

Sensing the swell of opposition, well-wishers of the reforms proposed an amendment. After five years with an outside majority under Lord Patten's chairmanship, congregation could decide whether it wished to restore to insiders a majority of eight to seven. This amendment was carried after a debate on 14 November, but it did nothing to appease opponents of the reforms. In the decisive debate on 7 December the new statute was thrown out by a vote of 730 to 456, and a few weeks later that rejection was confirmed by a postal vote in roughly the same proportions. For the time being, internal reform of Oxford's constitution is dead, and the university is governed by a council, and under a statute, which are regarded as unfit for purpose by both reformers and conservatives.

Chapter 5

How Oxford Works

In the present chapter I aim to set out which functions, in the collegiate university as at present constituted, are performed by the colleges, and which by the central university. I will try to explain where important decisions are taken.

Colleges and Halls

The colleges' oldest, and still very significant, function is to provide somewhere for students and dons to live. The colleges rightly resent it if they are described simply as halls of residence, but that is undoubtedly one of the things that they are. In the new millennium more students live in college than ever before, and fewer dons. Most dons are married and are not content to live in the bachelor suites that were the habitation of previous generations: they occupy studies in college, but live in housing elsewhere in Oxford (sometimes in houses owned by their college and allocated to them rent free). There are more student inhabitants of colleges not just because the number of junior members has increased (from ten and a half thousand in 1968 to 17,200 in 2003–4) but because undergraduates spend much more of their time inside colleges. In the mid-twentieth century few colleges could house their students for more than two years, and for the rest of their course they lived in private lodgings. In days when college discipline was rigid, with restricted visiting hours and strict gate curfews, young men and women were glad to live outside college, even in less comfortable billets. Now all that has changed. The relaxation of discipline has removed a deterrent from living in college, and in the last decades of the century most colleges have added modern buildings to their stock of accommodation. Some colleges have set themselves the target of accommodating all their students throughout their course, and many now provide married quarters for postgraduates. The Oxford landlady, as Chancellor Jenkins often sadly remarked while opening a new wing of a college, has become an almost extinct species.

The provision of living accommodation is almost entirely a college domain. Each college decides what buildings to erect and how to furnish and maintain them; each college decides who shall live in them and on what terms. The university maintains a number of blocks of graduate accommodation, but wishes to withdraw from this area; in addition it provides are a few houses for senior university officers and transitional accommodation for newly arrived professors.

Each college maintains its own separate catering establishment. The Asquith commission, comparing the cost of living in Oxford to that in other universities, concluded that the colleges were highly inefficient as hoteliers, and as a result of its recommendations, from 1929 to 1963 the university was supposed to inspect college kitchens every three or five years. Nowadays domestic bursars are kept on their toes rather by intercollegiate competition. The competition is not for the custom of students (who if they wish to eat in hall have no choice but their own college, and who may anyway prefer to cook their own food or survive on meals from take-aways) but for the conference trade. For nearly half of each year much college accommodation is empty of students, and is instead occupied by a variegated series of gatherings that find Oxford a congenial venue. Profits from conferences enable student charges to be subsidised, and the degree of comfort conferenciers expect in their accommodation has markedly improved the general standard of undergraduate living.

The desire of colleges to expand their accommodation has sometimes led to keen competition between one college and another for newly vacated buildings or newly available sites for building. This is not only unseemly but inefficient, since it raises the price to be paid to third parties. However, the conference business has impressed on bursars the advantages of co-operation as well as competition. In 1991 an agreement was signed for the central marketing of conference accommodation, totalling some 5,000 beds, which then brought in an annual income of £6m.

Colleges, of course, offer more than board and lodging to their students. Much teaching takes place in tutors' rooms, and colleges provide lecture and seminar rooms for both college and university instruction. Every college has a library which is the first port of call for undergraduates studying for an honour school. Senior and junior common rooms provide the focus for collegiate social life, and nowadays every college has formal provision for both medical and psychological pastoral care. Most colleges have their own sports facilities, sometimes shared with other colleges, and sometimes at a distance from the colleges' main sites. The typical undergraduate who is not outstanding either academically or athletically will, on leaving, have a memory full of life lived in a college context, but comparatively few recollections of the use of university facilities.

Traditionally, the colleges have had control over admission to Oxford. Colleges, that is to say, control not only admission to their own societies, but to the university as a whole. No one can be matriculated (enrolled as a student of the university) unless already a member of a college and presented to the university by that college. To this day, those who wish to become undergraduates apply first and foremost to a college (though they may delegate to a computer, if they wish, the choice of college). To enter the university, they must be accepted by one or other college. For graduate admissions, application is made first of all to the relevant faculty of the university; but again, in order to be matriculated, the applicant must secure a place at a college. In some science departments this requirement is seen as a burden.

In recent years, in the interests of transparency to applicants, some modification of the admission procedures has been adopted. But the recent reforms have not substantially reduced the overwhelming influence exercised by colleges in the admission of undergraduates. Nor should it, most people would say: it is one of the defining strengths of Oxford that students are admitted, not by some impersonal admissions bureaucracy, but by the tutors who will have the duty of personally teaching those that they have admitted.

The system however leaves one enormous gap: no one has effective authority to decide how many students Oxford should take. From time to time the central university sets targets, or limits, for the overall number, and some faculties, especially laboratory-based ones, impose caps on the number of students they will accept. But overall limits need to be negotiated with colleges and their observation has to be carefully monitored. There is nothing to prevent a college admitting students over quota provided that it can teach and house them, and once they have been admitted they can make use of all the university's facilities. In theory, the university could refuse to matriculate students from a college judged to be admitting irresponsibly. However, in the one case when the university threatened to use this power — in order to prevent the male colleges from stampeding to admit women—it proved impossible to carry out the threat. And if a college admits fewer students than the university thinks desirable, the university cannot compel it to take more.

Having admitted undergraduates, colleges then perform their most valuable role: they provide tutorial teaching. Most colleges have traditionally aimed to have their own undergraduates taught by their own fellows. Pupils might be sent for a term to a tutor in another college for specialist teaching, or entrusted for tutorials to graduate students when a fellow was overburdened. But such farming out was always the exception rather than the rule. Moreover, relations between pupil and tutor were understood to be more than merely academic: tutors might join students in sporting activities, or entertain them in their homes, or take them on reading parties during vacations. One hears that these ideals are threatened from various quarters. Governmental insistence on research productivity, and the compliance demands of various regulatory bodies, leave dons less time for teaching, let alone extra-curricular fraternising. Some tutors even question the academic efficiency of the one-on-one or two-on-one tutorial. But however trimmed the ideal may be, the tutorial system is still held up by both reformers and conservatives as a characteristic feature of Oxford's excellence which must not be allowed to wither away.

Colleges' relationships to their graduate students are not similarly close. A graduate student working for a taught master's course will depend mainly on seminars organised by the university, and a doctoral student working on a dissertation may have a supervisor in a quite different college. In general, colleges provide some minimal back-up, with the head of house or a tutor for graduates intervening when necessary to sort out any misunderstandings between a college member and the faculty authorities.

Even though they do not design courses or confer degrees, the colleges enjoy a considerable degree of academic self-government. They can decide for which of the disciplines offered by the university they will admit students: one college may decide it does not wish to teach foreign languages, another to abolish its theology school. A college, if it can find the funds, can decide how many teaching fellows it wishes to have in history or economics. It can create as many research fellows, or supernumerary fellows, as it can afford. It is only if it wishes a fellow to have a university post, or access to a university laboratory, that it will need to consult outside its own governing body.

Finally, colleges enjoy financial independence. They have complete control over their own endowments, and over the spending of whatever income they receive in fees and charges to students, or from grants from the university. (Colleges have never received funding directly from government; taxpayer support has been either through local authority payment of fees on behalf of students, or through HEFCE money channelled through the university).

University and faculties

So much for the prerogatives of the colleges. What, in this system, is controlled by the central university? The university determines, indirectly, the content of college teaching. In shorthand, it can be said that the university determines what courses are to be taught. But Oxford undergraduates do not follow courses in the sense in which a course is understood in most other universities, namely as a prescribed series of classes linked with exercises to be graded by the teacher. The way in which the university exercises control over college teaching is by imposing, at different stages during a student's residence, examinations which will have to be passed in order to obtain a degree. The precise manner in which undergraduates will be prepared for these examinations remains a matter for the individual college to decide.

Each faculty will draw up a list of topics to be examined, and will specify the information to be acquired, the texts to be studied, and the skills to be exhibited, as a condition of passing the examination. It will be the examination statutes for any given year that will determine the principle content of teaching in each of the colleges of the university. Those statutes are all that Oxford has in the shape of a syllabus.

Having drawn up the syllabus in this way, the faculty will then nominate a set of examiners (commonly drawn from a variety of colleges) to mark the examination papers and grade the candidates, placing them in one of the four possible classes of each honour school. The faculty is also responsible for appointing supervisors and examiners for postgraduate courses and doctoral dissertations.

Like examinations, lectures and seminars are a university responsibility, not a college one. In addition to lectures on the subjects prescribed for examinations, the university administers a large number of endowed visiting lectureships. Most lectures in most subjects are optional, and no census is taken of those attending. No formal inquiry is made to ascertain whether the university lectures offered to undergraduates coincide with, conflict with, or complement the teaching they are receiving in college. Some regard this as a scandal; others welcome it as discouraging students from swearing by the words of any one master.

The university provides the teaching and research facilities that are beyond the resources of individual colleges. There are the great research libraries that have been built over the centuries, such as the Bodleian and the Taylorian, and there are the art collections in the Ashmolean and the scientific collections in the University Museum. In the early twentieth century colleges were the first off the mark to provide laboratories in physics and chemistry, but the progress of these disciplines, and the direction of government funding, has meant that only the central university can afford to construct the laboratories, and provide the computing facilities, required by twenty-first century science. The largest scientific division is that of medical sciences, and this is funded by the university, in conjunction with the NHS, on a number of campuses in Oxford suburbs.

The most important function of any university is the recruitment and remuneration of academic staff, and here the responsibilities are shared between university and colleges. The most senior academics, the professors, are paid entirely by the university, and they are recruited by search committees appointed by the university, which will include two external experts, and two members of the college to which the chair is attached. Most appointments at a lower level are joint appointments: the remuneration is shared between university and colleges, and the appointing bodies will contain members from both sides, without external representation. If the post is in a scientific subject, the university's proportion both of electors and of salary will commonly be the greater, in a scientific subject; in an arts appointment the college will predominate. In all cases, each side has a veto, rarely exercised; there are elaborate procedures to be followed if such an impasse is reached. All joint appointments at a given level are paid on the same scale, with a maximum imposed on the total joint salary, though colleges have some latitude on the auxiliary inducements they can offer.

In all such joint appointments, the university will be dealing with a single college. In matters where the common concerns of the colleges have to be considered, the university has to negotiate with a conference of colleges, consisting of two members from each college. This unwieldy body has rarely been effective, since it has no power to bind its members, and individual colleges can nullify collective action. During its history it has often demonstrated that each college's autonomy is also a fetter on the liberty of other colleges.

A brief description of the Oxford system suffices to bring out its complexity. With forty autonomous decision-making centres there are two obvious dangers: duplication and conflict. In some areas duplication is no doubt wasteful, but it can also be seen as a positive merit. It is no bad thing that there should be many independent gates to admission and many different ways of preparing for examinations. Conflict is another matter: but surely, given that all forty bodies have a common overarching goal of education and the advancement of learning, any conflict should be easily resolved by people of good will. This should hold particularly given that in any potential conflict between university and colleges, the adversaries are not only persons of good will but to a great extent the very same persons wearing different hats.

In succeeding chapters we will try to identify how well or ill the collegiate university copes with these dangers of duplication and conflict.

Chapter 6

The Merits of a
Collegiate University

Recent debates about the governance of Oxford University focussed on the composition of the reformed university council. There was far less discussion of the other element of the proposed bicameral system, the new academic board. This was unfortunate, because the new academic board was intended to address the most serious problem in the management of Oxford's affairs: the difficulty of co-ordinating the activities of the colleges and of the central university. In this chapter and the next we propose to stand back and look at the advantages and disadvantages of being a collegiate university.

There is no doubt that Oxford's colleges inspire great loyalty in their members, junior and senior, present and past. Harold Macmillan when Chancellor delivered, on many occasions and in many places, a speech whose theme was that loyalty to small bodies was easier than loyalty to large bodies. "It is easier to love a regiment than an army, to love a College than to love a University". The sentiment was applauded in many a college hall.

Each college has its individual history and traditions. Some fortunate societies possess grand historic buildings, but even the mediocre architecture of the average college quickly inspires affection among its members. College societies, teams, and chapels forge bonds tighter than those across the wider campus.

Of course, all good universities inspire loyalty in their members, and cherish that loyalty with reunions and homecomings. But my impression is that Macmillan was right, and that college loyalty is something warmer and stronger than the normal loyalty to the university of one's youth. Certainly loyalty to Oxford colleges trumps loyalty to Oxford university.

A collegiate university, at its best, enables an individual member to enjoy the domestic warmth of a small liberal arts college while benefiting from the research capabilities of a large international institution. These benefits are felt at both junior and senior level.

Internal benefits

Junior members of colleges enjoy a greater degree of intensive individual teaching than students at non-collegiate universities. Traditionally, such teaching has been accompanied by friendly informal and pastoral relationships between pupil and tutor.

The small scale of the institutions enables those without great sporting or athletic abilities, who could never hope to represent their university, to play or swim or row at the level of intercollegiate competition. Shared college membership gives an undergraduate an opportunity to make friends in other disciplines; attendance at university lectures and classes brings acquaintances from the same discipline in other colleges. The endowments of colleges enable them to provide a degree of comfort for their junior members superior to that enjoyed by most students in the UK university system.

Senior members enjoy similar advantages. Many dons work in elegant and comfortable studies, and college senior common rooms are far more attractive than the average faculty club. The tutorial relationship has much to offer the tutor as well as the pupil, and can blossom into a lifelong friendship. In the years of worldwide student revolt, Oxford suffered much less than many other great universities. This was partly because the distinction between colleges meant that there were not monolithic blocks of students, faculty, and administration to go head to head with each other. Even at the height of the troubles there were many occasions on which Lazarus dons and Lazarus students had more in common with each other than either had with Dives dons and Dives students.

Intercollegiate competition can be a stimulus to good teaching. For many years a league table has been published (sometimes officially, sometimes clandestinely) showing how well or badly the members of each college has fared in the final examination. The scientific value of these tables is questionable, since small differences between positions in the league are rarely statistically significant. But if in a particular year a college moves sharply down the table, this leads to considerable self-examination by the college's tutors.

In matters of academic research, too, the college system has much to offer a don. Shared membership of common room and governing body offers the opportunity to form close friendships with scholars and scientists in other disciplines. It must be confessed that the intellectual opportunities thus offered are not fully exploited. Ralf Dahrendorf recalls that a senior businessman whom he took into a senior common room whispered in awe "it would be wonderful to know what all these intellectual high-fliers are talking about". "I can tell you" said Dahrendorf "money, money". But most dons can recall interdisciplinary enterprises which owed their origin to common room conversations, and later bore fruit on a wider academic stage.

Because colleges are not solely institutions for teaching and research, a fellowship provides opportunities for acquiring non-academic experience in the course of one's duties – as gardenmaster or investment bursar, as a member of the portraits committee or the estates committee, as a wine steward or as overseer of a building project. The variety of tasks offered by a college offsets the repetitive nature of much tutorial teaching and prevents a fellow's life from becoming monotonous.

Perhaps the most precious benefit that membership of a collegiate university has to offer an academic is a sense of autonomy. As a fellow of a college, a don reports only to a governing body of which he or she is a member: the head of a house is in no way a chief executive. As a member of the university, a don's ultimate responsibility is to congregation – again, a body to which he or she belongs. I remember, when first appointed to a fellowship, telling my friends "the great thing about Oxford is that you don't have a boss". The theme was constantly repeated in the recent governance debates. "In Oxford, nobody tells you what you have to do." Several speakers said that this autonomy was what attracted them to take a post in Oxford which might well pay less than their previous job. This is why talk of "line management" or of a "senior management team" sets the teeth of many dons on edge.

The confederacy

So far I have been talking entirely of the benefits that a college confers on its own members. Let us now ask: what do colleges offer to the university, and what does the university offer to the colleges?

The colleges undertake, for the university, the principal workload of undergraduate teaching. The intensive teaching offered in colleges underpins a large part of Oxford's educational reputation. The colleges also provide social facilities for Oxford's students at a standard that no non-collegiate university in the UK can afford. The congenial atmosphere of the colleges attracts highly qualified faculty members who might otherwise be put off by Oxford's uncompetitive salary scales. The loyalty of alumni to colleges brings into the collegiate university benefactions from donors which the central university, on its own, could never reach.

But if the colleges give much to the university, it can be said that the university gives everything to the colleges. It is not just that the central university provides research facilities that no college could afford by itself: it is that no college, taken apart from the whole Oxford confederation, could hope to preserve its identity, any more than a living cell can survive if removed from the body to which it belongs. Even the most distinguished college, if placed in isolation in the Isle of Man, would soon disappear off the spectrum of international higher education.

All this should go without saying, were it not that it seems to be called in question by some recent enthusiasts for college autonomy. To be fair, what they have in mind when they question the benefit conferred on colleges by the university is not any transplantation of colleges, but rather the amputation of parts of the university. Without an expensive medical faculty and a business school and some of the more elaborate science departments, they claim, Oxford would be freed from its current financial problems and could settle down, as a confederation of liberal arts colleges, to concentrate on what it does best, undergraduate education. Princeton—which already enjoys a special partnership with Oxford—is sometimes held up as a transatlantic model that might be imitated here.

If the underfunding of Oxford continues at recent rates, it may well be that such a scenario would be the best available option. But it is surely a counsel of despair. An Oxford shorn of major research enterprises would be a much less interesting place to work in and would quickly tumble from its place near the top of the international academic hierarchy.

Let us now look beyond both colleges and university, and ask to what extent Oxford's idiosyncratic system benefits the nation as a whole. Obviously, the nation needs universities, and good ones rather than bad. So whether Oxford's structure benefits the nation depends on whether a collegiate university, other things being equal, is better than a non-collegiate one, and if so, whether this advantage is worth the extra demands it makes on public money. It is, no doubt, a legitimate matter of national pride that Oxford and Cambridge are not only two of the world's most famous tourist attractions, but also score very highly in international academic league tables. But it is not obvious that it is in the national interest that two out of the UK's universities should be so much more comfortably funded than the remaining hundreds. The sight of the glories of Oxbridge may arouse envy rather than pride among those who can only bask in them from a distance. To ensure a continuance of national benevolence it is essential that Oxford should manage its own affairs in such a way as to demonstrate that its idiosyncratic system is the necessary underpinning of a first-class educational offering.

Chapter 7

The Drawbacks of the College System

The benefits of the college system are great. But the system brings with it disadvantages at every level — for undergraduates, for graduate students, for fellows, and above all for the university and for the world outside. We do not believe that these demerits outweigh the merits, nor that they are all necessary accompaniments of collegiality. But we think that they should be stated and evaluated with a clear eye.

Undergraduates in most universities can choose to take courses from any faculty member who teaches the subject they wish to study. Undergraduates in Oxford can likewise listen to the appropriate lectures from dons belonging to any college. But in the matter of tutorials they do not have a similarly unfettered choice. In general undergraduates are taught by tutors in their own college, and they may find themselves tied to a mediocre teacher while there is a charismatic star in the college next door. Arrangements, of course, can be made for a brilliant student from omega college to be sent out to a brilliant teacher at alpha college, but given the structure of the university such arrangements must be exceptional.

Graduate students when seeking a supervisor are not similarly limited to dons in their own college. If they are supervised by a professor, they and their fellow graduates will have first claim on her attention. However, it is also quite possible that the supervisor will turn out to be a college fellow whose primary responsibility will be to give undergraduate tutorials to the junior members of his own college.

Since college teaching is centrally determined only by the content of the papers in mid-career or final examinations, different parts of the syllabus may be taught in different terms in different colleges. In many subjects, no system exists for co-ordinating the content of university lectures with that of college tutorials. An undergraduate may have tutorials on a particular text, or on a particular historical period, some terms before or after the corresponding university lectures are given.

The collegiate system places some extra burdens on faculty members as well as on students. The tutorial method is demanding. I have taught classes of different sizes in several universities in the US and have always found a week of American teaching far less exhausting than a week spent giving Oxford tutorials. In a class the initiative is with the teacher, who controls the area to be covered, can prepare fully in advance, and can anticipate the students' likely responses. A tutor, on the other hand, will hear essays on many different topics in a single week, and a great deal of reading will need to be revisited if he is to be properly prepared. In each tutorial the initiative is with the pupil, not the tutor, and the better the pupil the more unpredictable will be the approach to the subject.

In an age when academics are pressed to produce publishable research, tutorial fellows may feel at a disadvantage. It is not a simple matter of college teaching taking up a great deal of time: Oxford does, after all, offer ample months of vacation. The problem is a different one. In most universities an academic can adopt a comparatively narrow field of study, read everything published within that field, teach courses based on that reading, and produce original research in the same area. In Oxford, because most of the colleges compete with each other to teach the whole range of subjects offered in the university, a college tutor is perforce a generalist, and specialised research must be a distinct and extra task.

The effect of this has been an increased demand by fellows for sabbatical and research leave, and for teaching buy-outs. Experiments are being made with less laborious methods of teaching. Tutors at the present time seem to be more aware of the demerits of the tutorial system, and less aware of its merits, than the tutors of a generation ago.

But the disadvantages that the collegiate system places on individuals are minor compared with the ones that the confederal structure places on the colleges themselves as institutions. College independence means that each college must put in place a complete administrative system, so that across Oxford there are thirty nine different structures replicating each other with only minor differences. Co-operative links between colleges have become commoner, but have not achieved significant economies of scale nor exploited to the full the massive purchasing power of the total confederation.

The administrative burden on colleges has been increased in recent years because of the ever-growing mass of regulation imposed by legislation. As one head of house put it "Health and safety, anti-discrimination, employment and data protection laws are four horsemen of the apocalypse galloping through the groves of academe". Each college has to put in place its own compliance regime. No wonder that many offices — such as that of bursar or senior tutor — which were formerly held as part-time posts by tutorial fellows are now being turned over in many colleges to professionals.

A sense of fraternity, in itself admirable, has meant that colleges, whatever their wealth, long ago agreed to pay their fellows on a single uniform scale. This means that financially the collegiate confederation is a convoy sailing at the speed of the slowest vessel — even if the college contributions system means that some of the faster ships give a modest tug to some of the slower ones. Thus it is intercollegiate solidarity, as much as anything else, that has kept Oxford salaries depressed for years.

The unanimous acceptance of the common salary scale is the more remarkable since there is no general mechanism for securing agreement between colleges, and on most other issues it proves difficult to achieve. No college can bind any other college, nor can a majority of colleges bind a minority, even a minority of one. In dealings with outside bodies, who may call for a binding decision, the confederation may be hamstrung by a single outrider.

But if the colleges collectively cannot control their members, still less can the university speak for all or any of the colleges. Any university decision which affects the colleges needs to be ratified by thirty nine governing bodies, which meet perhaps thrice a term. These will report back to the conference of colleges which meets just once in each term. This mechanism puts a most effective brake on reaching any verdict on any proposal.

In ecclesiastical circles there used to be a saying "canonici boni viri, capitulum mala bestia": the canons are good men, but the chapter is a foul beast. Colleges sometimes behave in a way reminiscent of this adage. The fellows are individually rational and well-intentioned, but collectively they are capable of reaching wrong headed decisions: and even if a decision is not wrong headed it may be a different right headed decision from the one reached by the college next door. And just as a collective of sound fellows may misbehave in a way that none of them would individually, so may a collective of colleges behave in a way that damages each college in the collective.

To give an indication of the way in which the multiplicity of colleges can bring decision-making to a grinding halt, I quote a recent minute of the university's governing council (now publicly available thanks to recent transparency regulations).

It concerns the need to agree on the way to distribute funds between the divisions and colleges, the JRAM or joint resource allocation method.

> At its meeting yesterday (March 12 , 2007) Council:
>
> 1.1. Noted that the timetable for decision making on the JRAM had been delayed by the Conference of Colleges which agreed in its meeting in Fifth Week not to take a decision until the Fifth Week meeting in Trinity Term. Council will not make its decision until the conference has deliberated and voted: in practice this means that Council will not be in a position to make a final decision until Michaelmas Term.
>
> 2. Agreed that the delay in agreeing the JRAM means that it will not be possible administratively to implement it for 2007–8, since budgets for the 2007–8 financial year will need to be set and agreed very soon. The earliest date for implementation is now 2008–9.

The hapless members of the Joint Resource Allocation Working Group may have another heavy year ahead of them.

This is just one, typical, instance of how the multiplicity of colleges, and the lack of a method of enforcing an agreement between them, can hold up indefinitely a matter of urgent importance to all of them. This instance concerned an internal issue, but dealings with external bodies are subject to similar procrastination. When the university receives a proposal from a funding body, or an inquiry from government or a regulatory body, the delay in responding can be very damaging to the interests of the entire collegiate university.

Individual colleges can not only prevent the collegiate university from making decisions: they can force on the university decisions that it does not wish to take. A faculty may decide that it needs to appoint a specialist in a particular field within a discipline. To do so, however, it needs to find a college association for the post, and no college may be willing to be associated with the post. Each college's desire to present itself as a micro-university means that it will seek posts, and appoint tutors, who work in areas regarded as central, rather than marginal, to the discipline. In the heyday of Oxford ordinary language philosophy, for instance, the faculty contained a score of lecturers on Plato and Aristotle, and more than a score who could teach Descartes, Locke, Berkeley and Hume, but only one or two mathematical logicians, and not a single specialist in either medieval or modern continental philosophy.

The financial autonomy of the colleges has as a consequence that income arriving in Oxford is not necessarily spent in the best interests of the entire collegiate university. While academic staff across the entire university complain of being underpaid, individual colleges may devote surplus funds to putting up an extra squash court, or yet another theatre for undergraduate drama. Facilities that a university of the size of Oxford might expect to enjoy may be lacking because they are not sufficiently essential to have a claim on an impoverished university, while being too large for an individual college to provide. It was decided long ago that there should be a university swimming pool: but it took thirty years, and generous outside benefactions, to persuade the colleges to dig into their pockets and make appropriate contributions to the cost of building a pool. To this day, though colleges provide many bijou venues for chamber music, neither the university nor the city of Oxford has a concert hall suitable for a symphony orchestra.

In all universities there are tensions between the needs for teaching and the demands of research. In all universities there are tensions between the structures appropriate for the pursuit of arts and social studies, and the structures needed for investigations in experimental science. In Oxford these tensions can be exacerbated between the colleges, which concern themselves principally with teaching, mainly in humane subjects, and the university, which is responsible for providing the facilities for research in the hard sciences. These tensions seem set to increase as more and more of Oxford's scientific work is carried out by workers on short-term research contracts who enjoy none of the benefits of collegiate life but suffer from the constraints which the college system imposes on the university.

Chapter 8
Oxford in Financial Terms

Introduction

Getting an aggregate picture of Oxford's financials is complex. The individual colleges do now publish clear, audited accounts, and the university has done so for some time. However, since the colleges are not in any legal sense subsidiaries of the university, their figures are not consolidated into the university accounts. Beyond certain headline figures there are also no aggregate numbers for the colleges. Thus the only way to get a complete picture is to combine the individual college and university figures.

Since funds flow between the colleges and university, and between the colleges themselves, there is a risk of double-counting in aggregating the figures. However, we have corrected for the 'College Capitation Payment' (the flow-through of HEFCE funds from the university to the colleges) and the redistribution of funds between colleges through the College Contribution Committee, and so believe that the figures that follow represent a fair overall picture.

We have however excluded from our calculations the seven permanent private halls associated with the university that do not have college status. We have also excluded the revenue and costs of Oxford University Press, though we have included in university income a donation of £35m made by OUP in 2005/06. The university figures below also include the financials of three smaller colleges, Green, Kellogg and St Cross, which are not separate and independent legal entities.

Oxford's income

On an aggregate basis the university and colleges had income of £804m[1]. Key sources were HEFCE (£166m), research grants (£216m) and transfers from endowments plus interest (£110m). In total £609m flowed in the first instance to the university.

HEFCE is the Higher Education Funding Council for England, a government funded body that in 2005/06 distributed over £6bn to English universities and colleges. It provides money for research, teaching and other purposes. In 2005/06 £90m (well over half) of the HEFCE grant to Oxford was for research, and £59m was for teaching[2]. Of this, £41m flowed through to the colleges. The university is not obliged by HEFCE to pass this money through, but has chosen to do so.

HEFCE allocates funding between the English institutions in a variety of ways. Grants are partially driven by student numbers and research quality, but some funds are for special purposes such as widening access or maintaining old buildings.

In addition to the research component of the funds from HEFCE, the university received a further £213m of research grants, which were roughly evenly split between research councils, charities and other sources. The research councils are another government funding mechanism, disbursing £2.8bn annually across the UK. In Oxford in 2005/06 they supported research into everything from the impact of early star formation on the protogalactic environment to landscape and gender in nineteenth-century Italian opera.

The final key source of funding was transfers from endowments. Oxford has an aggregate endowment of £3.0bn, mostly held by the colleges. If Oxford were a public company, even if it had no value beyond its endowment, this sum would entitle it to a place in the FTSE 100[3]. Oxford endowments are typically managed so that they can at least retain their values in real terms after using 3% to 4% of their total for operating or other needs in a given year. In 2005/06 Oxford spent 3.0% of its year-end endowment (or 3.2% of the year-start endowment). However the value of its aggregate endowment grew by over £300m net of this spend, thanks to a rising stock market and new donations.

[1] Unless stated otherwise, all figures in this chapter are from the authors' analysis of the university and individual college accounts, 2005/06
[2] HEFCE *Recurrent Grants* at
  http://www.hefce.ac.uk/pubs/hefce/2005/05_43/
[3] Based on market capitalisations as of 16th March 2007. Oxford valued at 0% discount to combined NAV of endowment at end 2005/06

In addition to these key income streams, Oxford received smaller amounts from a plethora of other sources. These include: room rents and meal charges from students; conference fees; the Oxford University Press; an intellectual property licencing deal for the output of the chemistry department; and the profits of the Lamb and Flag pub, owned by St Johns.

University and colleges compared

At least from the perspective of income and expenditure the university dominates the aggregate picture. Even without the College Capitation Payment, the university receives 71% of the income, the colleges 29%. Of course, any single college would receive far less. However, in terms of wealth, the university's endowment of £629m at the end of 2005/06 is a fraction of the colleges' £2,419m.

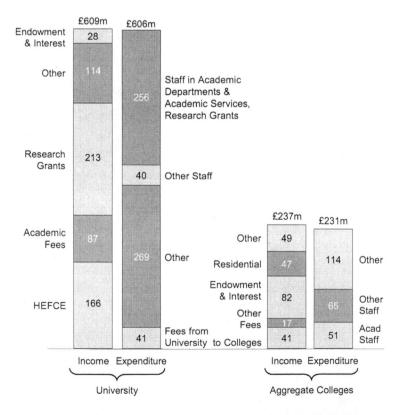

University and College Income and Expenditure, 2005/06 (£m)

The university's balance sheet does not include any value for the OUP, but this could be considered to be part of the university's endowment. OUP had a surplus after tax of £71m for the year ending March 2006, on revenue of £448m. If we were to apply a price to earnings ratio of 17.8 to this (equivalent to the average of Pearson, Bloomsbury and Reed Elsevier[4]), then we get a value of £1.25bn for the OUP. Alternatively we can estimate the endowment equivalent by applying the 3% yield charities expect (conservatively) to draw from their endowment. Dividing this into the £35m OUP transferred to the university gives a value of £1.17bn, by coincidence a very similar figure. Adding the former figure to the £629m cash endowment gives a total of £1.88bn, still appreciably below the £2.42bn held by the colleges, and as we will discuss below we believe there is significant off-balance sheet value in the college buildings.

Of course other universities have their own academic presses, but they generally lose money. OUP is an important and rare asset.

Research and teaching

The public perception of Oxford is primarily shaped by its teaching role. This is certainly the function that attracts most attention from the press and government ministers. More strictly it is admissions that gets the attention. Once students arrive at the university, their doings are largely ignored, unless they involve a drug overdose, the boat race or a retrospective review of a politician's undergraduate years.

However, the financials tell a different story. Here it is research that dominates, not teaching. If we combine the research grants and the portion of the funds from HEFCE that are also for research, we get a total of £304m. This compares to income of £153m in college and university fees and the HEFCE allocation for teaching. Of course one of Oxford's challenges is that its teaching is loss making (to a greater extent than research, in general), and so the income for these functions is not a fair reflection of the relative activity involved. However, even if we assume the whole purpose of endowment income is to subsidise the teaching loss, we get a total income of £265m for teaching, still less than the £304m for research.

Staff numbers tell the same story. Oxford has approximately 1,400 academics who teach or teach and research, compared to 2,300 who

---

[4]   Weight average PE of 17.8 as of 1 March 2007. Author's analysis of data from Interactive Investor

only research[5]. Of course teaching is absolutely central to Oxford, but any discussion of the optimal Oxford that is based solely on an image of a college don and student in a tutorial will miss a very large part of the picture. It needs to be balanced by the white-coated researcher at her microscope. Fully 65% of externally funded research grants and contracts (which excludes HEFCE research funds) is for the medical sciences, and one third of the university's income comes from this division. A further 25% of research grants goes to mathematical and physical sciences[6].

Does Oxford provide value for money?

The government is Oxford's largest 'customer'. HEFCE and research council grants total £237m, or 30% of income. This substantial but not complete dependence on the government puts Oxford in an awkward position. It is a private supplier of what is felt to be a public good, dealing with a government that has the inclination and (through its funding) the leverage to intervene.

Dons may find that the executives from BT, Thames Water and British Gas share their pain when it comes to the aggravations of unwarranted government intrusion. At least with those institutions the government has the excuse that it is still managing the migration from monopoly provision. Oxford lost its monopoly in 1209.

How can we test whether the government is getting value for money from Oxford? According to one authoritative source, the cost to educate the average undergraduate is £18,600 per year, versus income of £9,500[7] (2002/03 figures), so that even if the value of the education was no more than the cost to provide it (an extreme view), the government would still be getting an excellent deal. From another perspective, colleges on average offset 34% of their costs using endowment and interest income. They would have to be fantastically inefficient for the government not to be getting good value. It is hard to imagine the government complaining if a commercial supplier offered it a 'cost-minus' contract, with the difference to be made up from shareholders funds.

---

[5]   HESA Reference Volume: Resources in Higher Education Institutions, 2004/05

[6]   Oxford University website,
       http://www.admin.ox.ac.uk/rso/statistics/ar_2005-06.shtml

[7]   Oxford University, *Oxford's Academic Strategy : A Green Paper*, February 2005

Of course, it is more reasonable to believe that the value of the Oxford degree is actually greater than the cost to provide it, though by its nature this value is hard to quantify. There are however parallels to the way in which the performance of the BBC is measured. The BBC receives approximately £3bn per year from the licence fee. To assess whether fee payers are getting value for money from this, the BBC conducts market research into its perceived value. They ask respondents what they feel the BBC set of services is worth to the average person. The aggregate UK value for the BBC in 2004 was £6,085m[8] compared to the licence fee of £2,798m. Dividing one into the other gives a 'value yield' for the BBC of 2.17x, providing substantial reassurance that the BBC is providing good value for money. (The British Library undertook a comparable exercise in 2003[9] and found it had a value yield of 4.4x).

To assess total value the BBC does not ask what the respondent would pay, since this can underestimate value, as impoverished respondents may give a low figure even though the services have great value to them. This lower value is known as the consumer value, and the difference between this and the total is known as the citizen value. Since the very justification of the BBC is that it generates positive externalities (wider benefits to society beyond those for which an individual consumer might pay) through the provision of content that the commercial sector would not supply, this distinction between citizen value and consumer value is important.

If we were to apply to Oxford the methodology used by the BBC, what might be the result? Short of substantial market research, we can't assess the value citizens might place on an Oxford degree. However, we can look at the purely economic value to the individual, in terms of the increase in lifetime earnings resulting from a tertiary qualification. This should be much lower than the citizen value, since it ignores the substantial intangible non-financial benefits to the graduate (including the undoubted pleasures of studying at Oxford), and also the benefits to society of better educated citizens.

The discounted value of increased lifetime earnings from a UK degree is £160,000[10] (compared to an individual with similar A-levels who does not go to university). We would hope that Oxford, with

[8] May 2004 research by the BBC and Human Capital, published in *Can the market deliver? Funding public service television in the digital age*, 2005
[9] Spectrum Strategy Consultants and Indepen, *Measuring the economic impact of the British Library*, 2003
[10] PriceWaterhouseCoopers for Universities UK, *The economic benefits of a degree*, February 2007

its highly qualified staff and low student to faculty ratio would do better than this. There is evidence to suggest that prestigious universities do outperform the average,[11] but let us use it as our basis for the citizen value, while acknowledging that it is probably greater than the consumer value in that not many students would be willing to pay this to attend. Against the £160,000 benefit the individual has fees to attend of £3,000 per year and foregone earnings of £10,000 per year. This gives a three year total cost of £39,000, and so a net benefit to the individual of £121,000.

This figure compares to the cost to the government of £4,900[12] for each of three years (for most degrees), or a total of £14,700. Dividing this figure into the £121,000 gives us a value yield of 8.2x. Of course this calculation and that for the BBC are not wholly comparable, but we should be reassured that this estimate for Oxford is giving a value yield that compares favourably to the Corporation's.

However, the practical reality is that even if the government is getting a very good deal from Oxford, that does not mean it will resist the temptation to intervene. It is also the case that the perspective of the government as a customer of Oxford getting a very good deal is not the only way to look at things. Oxford is not educating and researching because the government has asked it to. These are the very raisons d'être of the organisation. However Oxford requires a subsidy from the government to deliver the current quantum of research and education. It surely is legitimate for the government to seek to ascertain if Oxford is being run in such a way to minimize the public subsidy?

This argument stands even if you allow (as we do) that there are huge public benefits to tertiary education. There are huge public benefits to the provision of clean water, or telecommunications, but were the water companies or telcos to go cap in hand to the government for funds to cover a loss, I as a taxpayer would be keen that the government probe the need for and level of any hand-out. Indeed, this is precisely what telecoms regulators have done when authorising historic subsidies for the provision of service priced below cost to people in outlying regions.

---

[11] See Arnaud Chevalier & Gavan Conlon, *Does it pay to attend a prestigious university?*, March 2003

[12] Based on a HEFCE undergraduate teaching and ASN grant of £50.5m, cited in Oxford University, *A Joint Resource Allocation Method for the Collegiate University – Consultation Document*, Michaelmas Term 2006, and 10,364 UK/EU undergraduates

In an academic context it is extremely hard to assess value for money, since the outputs are inherently difficult to quantify. Notwithstanding the huge effort put into the Research Assessment Exercises (RAEs) which are used to allocate HEFCE research funds, it is not clear they have told us anything we didn't know already. Moreover, such mechanistic processes have encouraged people to game the system, much in the manner of police forces with crime reduction targets being reluctant to accept reports of offenses. For instance, Oxford has committed £11m "specifically to support research in preparation for the next RAE".

While it may be difficult to assess value for money, that does not undercut the legitimacy of the government's question. Further, if dons argue (rightly) that it isn't feasible to do a detailed assessment of output, then they leave the government little choice but to test value for money by looking at organisational inputs, such as the structure of the university.

The individual colleges

Thus far in this chapter we have treated colleges as an amorphous block, but of course they are in fact highly heterogeneous. This is evident in their financials. Annual expenditure ranges from Christ Church's £17m to Harris Manchester's £1.5m. Spend on academic salaries ranges from 8.6% of total non-depreciation costs at Linacre to 43% at Nuffield. Success at fundraising is unevenly distributed and varies from year to year, dependent on campaigns and the kind gifts of particularly lavish benefactors. In 2005/06 at one extreme Balliol raised £3.0m for its endowment, and at the other Nuffield and All Souls were in the luxurious position of not needing to raise a single penny. Endowments total £2.4bn, but range from Templeton's £1m to St John's £279m (by itself, equivalent to more than 40% of the university's endowment of £629m, and on a per student basis, equivalent to Stanford's, at £481,000).

The key to having a large endowment is to have been founded before 1620. All the colleges founded before this are richer than virtually all the colleges founded afterwards, with the graduate college of Nuffield the only significant richer newcomer, thus proving both the power of compound interest and the expense of teaching undergraduates.

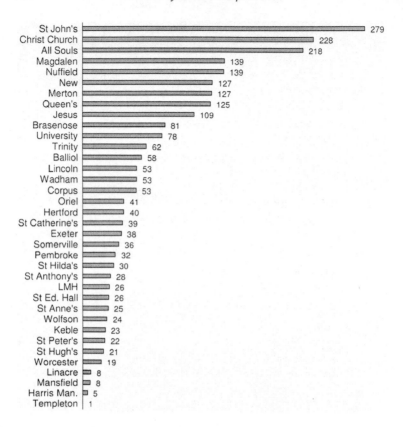

College endowments, July 31 2006 (£m)

The value of historic buildings

We would argue that the older colleges have another endowment advantage that does not appear in their accounts, namely their historic buildings. On the face of it, these are a burden. The older buildings are expensive to maintain and difficult to upgrade for modern conveniences such as en-suite showers and internet access. The 'hotel' side of the colleges tends to make a loss. If we take residential income from college members and conferences, and subtract residential, premise and catering costs we get an aggregate deficit for the colleges of £26m. (This calculation includes the cost of space for college office and teaching space in addition to accommodation, and therefore does somewhat overstate the 'hotel' loss. All organisations need office space, and accept this will be a cost centre.)

However, the colleges include some of the finest buildings in the UK, including many that are Grade I listed. (Oxford being Oxford, even Rymans and Tim's Newsagent's on the High occupy Grade II* listed buildings). The magnificence of these buildings does have some immediate financial benefits — they clearly support the colleges' conference business, and Christ Church was able to charge tourists in search of Hogwarts £745,000 in admission fees.

However, we feel the greater benefit from the buildings is in their attractiveness to both potential students and dons. The vast majority of students will never subsequently live in accommodation as distinguished as their university rooms (at least the years they live in), and many dons enjoy offices of greater area and infinitely greater character than do most CEOs. To appreciate the importance of the physical premises (if the point needs proving) one only need imagine the consequences if Oxford was moved to purpose built, functional, but anodyne accommodation somewhere outside the ringroad.

Can we quantify the benefit of this wealth of glorious buildings? Not with any accuracy, the market for second hand colleges having been somewhat illiquid of late. But let us try a very crude estimate. At the time of writing, an 8 bedroom Victorian house on Norham Gardens (a relatively central street, on the border of the University Parks) was on offer for £3.75m, or just under £0.5m per bedroom. While the bedrooms may be larger than the college average, this fine house is only Grade II listed, and not as central as most college accommodation, so let us take £0.5m as our per room benchmark.

Colleges founded before 1900 (that is, those with at least some buildings roughly as old as Norham Gardens) have in total 13,768 students. Let us assume two thirds of those live in, and a third of those are in older, distinguished rooms. That gives us 3,059 such rooms, and therefore a notional value of £1.5bn. This is almost three times the endowment of the university, and 70% of the total cash endowment of the colleges. To reiterate, this is obviously a very crude estimate, but is indicative of a massive asset Oxford has that is literally off balance sheet (since the ancient buildings have long since been fully depreciated), and important to its ability to attract the best junior and senior members. It is also an asset, like the cash endowments, that is very unevenly distributed between the colleges.

Existing mechanisms to address wealth differences

The colleges recognise their diversity of wealth, and seek to allow for it in two ways. Firstly there is the mechanism of the colleges contribution committee, which in essence taxes the richer colleges to subsidise the poorer through occasional grants. The tax is based on each college's endowment plus an imputed equivalent capital value of conference income. Taxation begins at a wealth of £30m and rises to a rate of 0.36% of wealth for those colleges with more than £39m. Given a 3% benchmark for transfers from the endowment for annual expenditure, this is equivalent to a top rate income tax of 12% on the benchmark transfer.

While this cross subsidy has provoked annual angst and occasional avoidance on the part of the richer colleges, the rate is set relatively low. The total 'tax' on the 23 paying colleges was £3.4m. St Johns, the largest contributor, paid £674,000 in 2005/06. This represented an additional operating cost of 5%, or 0.24% of the college's endowment.

This movement of funds is not particularly designed to equalise the wealth of the colleges, and it will not have this effect this century. The aggregate value of per-student endowment above the university median held by the richer colleges is £1,155m[13]. Ignoring for a moment the more rapid growth of the larger endowments, the current rate of redistribution would take 343 years to equalise the colleges' wealth.

Of course in practice the endowments of the richer colleges are growing faster in absolute terms than those of the smaller colleges because they are getting a return on a larger asset base. In 2005/06 St John's endowment rose £21.4m (after its College Contribution Scheme payment and use of funds for that year's operating expenses). Templeton, the college with the smallest endowment, actually saw a decrease of £120,000.

The second way the colleges handle their wealth divergence is by de facto self denying ordinances on the part of the richer colleges. Most critically, the richer colleges agree not to pay their dons more than those in the poorer colleges — the whole convoy moves at the speed of the slowest ship. Given the heterogeneity of wealth, this is a convoy that includes everything from ocean-going liners to coracles. The practical consequence of this is that the vast bulk of Oxford's endowment can not be used to make attractive financial offers to lure star academics, or keep the stars that are already in the firmament. (The Vice-Chancellor does have a degree of discretion in using university funds for this purpose at the professorial level).

---

[13] This figure excludes All Souls' endowment of £218m. All Souls has no undergraduates and only five graduates.

Instead the college endowments are used to increase the number of dons (certainly not a bad thing) or to erect new buildings for the greater comfort of students. This all makes perfect sense if your prime concern is the orderly management of competition between the colleges. If instead you are more concerned about competition between Oxford and other universities, it seems a bit odd.

There are exceptions to the leveled pay. Quality of college housing can be quite different for instance. Another stark example was New College's decision in 2006 to share with its fellows part of the proceeds from a £55m sale of land it had received from the Bishop of Winchester in 1386. Full fellows are to get £30,000 over three years, and junior fellows £7,500. David Palfreyman, the college's bursar, described the sale as "putting some jam on the college scone",[14] and given relatively low rates of academic pay, there is nothing inherently wrong with some jam redistribution to provide retention payments to staff. However, it is another example of the distorting effect of the fragmentation of the university. In an ideal world, at least from Oxford's perspective, such a sum would have been used to retain the most valuable and at-risk individuals in the university. Instead it was used to reward a certain set of dons for their wisdom in their choice of college, whether or not a given individual's departure would be an appreciable blow to the university.

Diseconomy of subdivision into colleges and responses

It is also hard to escape the feeling that the fragmentation of the non-academic functions of the colleges must carry an appreciable operating financial cost. Similar functions are being carried out in 39 different organisations, presumably with a smaller and less expert team, and purchases are being made in much less bulk than might be the case.

Looking purely at the direct administrative cost (which would exclude the impact of fragmentation on purchasing, for example), Oxford as a whole spends 7.3% of its expenditure on admin. For the aggregate colleges the figure is 7.6%, and for the university 6.7%. This compares to 4.7% to 7.7% for Bristol, Durham, Warwick and Bath[15], each far smaller institutions that might be expected to have a higher ratio. It may not be possible within the constraints of the collegiate system, but bringing Oxford's administrative spend ratio to the average of these four universities would free up £8m per year.

[14] Quoted in the *THES*, 26 May 2006
[15] Author's analysis of these universities' financial statements for 2005/06

The smaller colleges spend a far greater portion of their expenditure on administration. Harris Manchester and Linacre spend 15% or more, Univ, Christ Church and St Johns all spend less than 4%. Note that the figures for Oxford exclude the substantial time spent on admin by academic staff. If a typical don has half his cost covered by his college, and spends 5% of his time on college admin, then if we attributed his cost in proportion to administration, the average college spend on admin would rise 3 percentage points.

However, the colleges are increasingly co-operating with each other and with the university to make the most of their combined scale. For instance, a number of colleges have now deposited a portion of their endowments with the university for centralised investment management. In 2006 Balliol, Christ Church and St Catherine's jointly established Oxford Investment Partners, a new fund manager that will invest portions of these colleges' endowments, and were subsequently joined by New College and St Johns. The benefit of this combination of funds is more likely to accrue from a higher return (relative to risk) from a more diverse portfolio and access to new asset classes than from a reduction in expenses. In aggregate the colleges accounts show a £10m spend on managing their combined endowment of £2.4bn, but this presumably excludes external managers' charges directly against the funds.

Colleges also work with the university to maximise their conference income, through an association called Conference Oxford. However, there is as of yet no equivalent of the London Universities Purchasing Consortium to capture buying scale. The benefit of capturing this scale would need to be traded off against the administrative cost, particularly given the comparatively small spend of the colleges. Total non-staff, non-depreciation expense of the colleges was £89m. LUPC oversees £1bn.[16]

Academic pay

Academic pay in general has been a contentious issue, and many feel that is now at a dangerously low point. Certainly it has been falling relative to other occupations in recent decades. However, on a national level it is not self-evident that there is a problem in current relativities to other professions.

University teachers appear to be in with the field of similar professionals (and can count themselves fortunate that they are no longer

---

[16]   London Universities Purchasing Consortium, *Annual Report 2005–2006*

in clerical orders). They also enjoy an unusual benefit in the form of sabbaticals, the right to take one term in seven as paid leave, to teach elsewhere or write. However if instead we were to look at mean pay rather than median, we get a slightly different picture. Academics drop from 7th in this group to 17th. Unlike most other professions, there is not a core of highly paid leaders to pull the mean away from the median. National pay scales combined with a desire to maintain the republic of letters has kept academic pay in a comparatively narrow band — the national equivalent of the inter-college parity mentioned above.

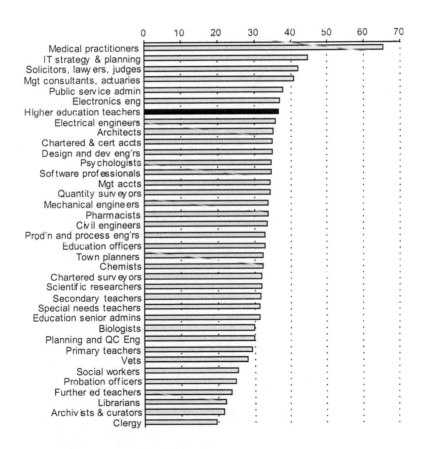

Median pay of UK professional occupations (£'000), 2006
Source: Annual Survey of Hours and Earnings, Office for National Statistics

Outside income can partially offset this. Overall 7% of academic staff in 2004 had additional earnings of more than £5,000[17], but 14% of business academics and 12% of computer scientists did so, narrowing the gap between academic and commercial pay for these individuals. (English literature, maths, physics and biology did least well, with only 3% or 4% of these academics breaking the £5,000 threshold).

Some Oxbridge dons cast an envious eye over the incomes of their students heading off to the City or top tier consultancies. This is an occupational hazard for the educators of elites. No doubt Aristotle muttered darkly about Alexander the Great's starting salary. While this is only human, we are not sure the comparison is particularly relevant. Only 6% of Oxford graduates go directly into investment banking or consulting[18], and academic jobs have offsetting advantages in job security and quality of life.

However we do believe there are real causes for concern regarding Oxford pay levels. That national academic salaries are perhaps reasonable is cold comfort to a junior don struggling with Oxford house prices that are 63% above the national average,[19] and indeed there is no shortage of anecdotal evidence to suggest that this is a real problem for recruitment.

The argument for better academic pay is also made in global context - Oxford is a world-class teaching and research institution, and it seems unlikely to continue to be so with pay that is merely average within the UK, and well below US figures. Average pay for academic staff at Oxford was estimated to be 34% below Princeton and 44% below Harvard in 2002/03.[20] Admittedly there is a general wealth difference between the US and the UK — in 2003 GDP per capita was 19% lower in the UK — but even allowing for this there is an appreciable pay difference.

---

[17] NIESR/DfES Staff survey, 2004, quoted in Hilary Metcalf, Heather Rolfe, Philip Stevens and Martin Weale, *Recruitment and Retention of Academic Staff in Higher Education*, National Institute of Economic and Social Research, 2005

[18] Oxford University, *Oxford Outline 2006*

[19] Halifax House Price Index, Q4 2006

[20] OxCHEPS and the Ulanov Partnership, *Costing, funding and sustaining higher education : A case study of Oxford University*, February 2004

However, there is not strong evidence that UK academic salaries are low by comparison to countries other than the US. A 2005 study[21] of nine developed economies showed that the UK was second only to the US in academic pay, and scored appreciably higher than any of the other eight countries in the ratio of academic pay relative to pay for the rest of the economy. These are surveys on a national basis and do not reflect pay differences between institutions in a given market. In countries with less leveled pay than the UK, certain more generous universities may have an advantage relative to Oxford. However, these national figures are consistent with the phenomenon we will discuss elsewhere of some flow of talent to the US from the UK, but appreciable flow in to Oxford from the rest of the world.

Alumni fundraising

In addition to moving away from leveled pay, we believe another opportunity for Oxford to realise more of its potential is through continued enhancement of its alumni fundraising. Both Oxford and Cambridge have been relatively successful in their fundraising relative to other UK universities, with alumni giving rates of around 10% versus a national average of 1%. However, US state universities typically have rates of 15% and Yale, Harvard and Princeton all achieve over 40%[22]. No doubt some of the gap is due to the greater wealth and philanthropic habit of America, but at least some Oxford alumni are surprised simply that they are not asked for money more often. They perhaps are unaware of the complex rules that Oxford has historically imposed on itself regarding such requests. Until 2006 these rules were structured to give the colleges priority over the university, which had to obtain clearance from a college before it could approach a given former member of that college for any substantial donation.

The new rules strike a more even balance between the colleges and university, and there may be benefit in going even further. Firstly, at least 31 of the colleges have a higher per-student endowment than the university, and that relative poverty should make the latter more zealous in its fundraising.

Secondly, it is axiomatic in fundraising that you would rather have a donation for a general purpose, rather than one tied to some-

[21] Hilary Metcalf, Heather Rolfe, Philip Stevens and Martin Weale, *Recruitment and Retention of Academic Staff in Higher Education*, National Institute of Economic and Social Research, 2005
[22] Sutton Trust, *University Fundraising – An Update*, December 2006

thing specific. By definition any donation for a particular college is less useful to Oxford than a donation for general purposes. Moreover, presumably the marginal value of a pound to a poorer institution is greater than its marginal value to a richer one.

The hypothecation problem

To illustrate the 'general purpose' point, imagine if when you received your pay cheque you immediately had to split it into different bank accounts each of which could only be used for one kind of spending — say food, rent, or utilities. Having assigned the money, it could only be moved from one account to another at a rate of 0.5% per year (the approximate rate of transfer from rich to poor colleges). Unless you were receiving a salary far in excess of your spending, financial disaster would shortly follow.

The counter to this metaphor would be that the better parallel for Oxford is to a group of individuals, each with their own salaries and own (single) accounts. Of course there is no intermingling of funds between them. But we believe that the university and the colleges thrive or fail together, and therefore an aggregate approach should be our starting point.

To get a financial perspective on this, let us assume, arbitrarily, that the marginal value of a pound of endowment in a college with more than the median per-student endowment is half that of a pound in a poor college. By value here we mean utility in achieving Oxford's overall teaching and research objectives. The aggregate college endowment above the per-student median is £1,155m. If half of this value is 'latent', then redistribution could have a £577m benefit. This is obviously purely illustrative, but gives a sense of the potential scale.

The richer colleges are not simply sitting on their endowments. They are spending from them at broadly similar percentage rate as the college average. Thus an implication of our above assumption on marginal value must be that they are spending on items that are not optimal from Oxford's perspective. We do in fact believe this is true. A prime example would be new undergraduate lodgings. Student accommodation in the richer colleges already compares very well to that available at other UK universities, so such spending can do little to improve the quality of Oxford's applicants (though it might improve a particular college's). If the accommodation is offered to students at less than the market rate, then it represents a subsidy to students at a time when Oxford would like to be receiving more money from its undergraduates, not less. It is also a particularly blunt form of subsidy, benefiting the rich and the poor student equally.

In the constructing colleges' defence, we should note that the City Council expects Oxford to accommodate 83% of its students,[23] a target that has not been met.

Conclusion

In financial terms Oxford is a substantial organisation, one that would in any case represent an appreciable management challenge. The challenge is all the greater given Oxford's subdivision into at least 40 autonomous units. Nonetheless it appears to be providing good value to its 'customers'. In the next chapter we will discuss whether this is because of or in spite of Oxford's organisational structure.

---

[23] Oxford University, *Corporate Plan 2005-6 to 2009-10*, July 2005

Chapter 9

An Outside Perspective on Oxford's Structures

Oxford conservatives worry about barbarians at the gate. But if non-academic outsiders, and in particular people with commercial backgrounds, were given some role in the governance of the university, how might they use it? Would they be barbarians like Attila at Aquileia, with barely a stone left on stone? Or more like Theodoric in Ravenna, a revitalising force? It is worth looking at how the barbarians manage similar organisations within their own kingdoms.

Organisations dependent on highly skilled professionals

Oxford 'adds its value' primarily through its highly skilled staff, the academics. It is not like a telecoms company, creating value through capital invested in its network, or many clothing manufacturers, where the cheapest possible labour is of the essence. Nor is it based around the constant honing of a particular process, such as Dell's focus on moving rapidly devaluing electronics components from their suppliers to their customers (in the form of completed PCs) as quickly as possible.

However, there are many commercial organizations that are just like Oxford in being primarily dependent on highly skilled individuals. Law firms, management consultancies, venture capital firms, architecture practices and advertising agencies would all be examples. For such firms, the loss of a set of key individuals would be a crippling blow—the company would simply cease to exist. This is quite different from the situation in GE or Boots, say. While they would be distressed if their senior team were to suddenly retire en masse, much of the day to day operations of these companies would carry on regardless.

Firms that are so dependent on their professional staff take care to retain them. They need to be thoughtful about what attracts and repels such individuals. In certain cases they solve this problem bluntly by throwing huge sums of cash at them — investment banks being a prime example — but most companies, like Oxford, do not have this option.

Instead, they provide a pleasant working environment, career progression, and most relevantly a say in the running of the firm. Many such companies are partnerships. In a partnership, the partners share collective responsibility for the success of their organisation. They jointly review finances, determine strategy and decide on new members of the partnership. There may be a first amongst equals - a founding partner or managing partner - but it would be an unwise or desperate such primus inter pares that attempted to ram change down the throats of his partners. Very often the managing partner is elected by the partnership.

Why do professional service firms structure themselves in this way? Certainly it isn't because this is the most efficient way to make decisions, at least not in the narrow stopwatch-and-clipboard sense. Partnership decision making can be long, repetitive and indecisive. (If the parallels to the collegiate system weren't already obvious, perhaps they are now).

Partnerships structure themselves as such because they recognise that their professional staff are vital to what they do; that these individuals have other career options; and that participation in decision making is an extremely important part of job satisfaction. They trade off decision making inefficiency against the ability to attract and retain the best people.

This is not to say that only highly trained professionals get satisfaction from participation in wider decision making, but rather to say that within businesses that are highly dependent on them, they have the leverage to obtain it. More junior, replicable employees may not be able to bargain for such participation, though in Oxford often even the newest fellow qualifies for participation in college decision making.

In situations where the professionals too lack bargaining power, the organisational outcomes can be very different. In the command economy of the Soviet Union in 1979 the eye surgeon Dr Svyatoslav Fyodorov introduced the surgical conveyor, an assembly line for the treatment of myopia. Individual doctors spend the entire day repeatedly performing one single step of the operation (making incisions on the cornea, for instance), before the patients glide along the conveyor belt to the next surgeon.

While this is highly efficient, treating more than 1,000 patients per day in a single facility, it is hard to imagine professionals with many other options putting up with such a mechanical, repetitive job. Certainly few if any Western organisations, commercial or public, have tried to introduce it.

The trade-off between decision making efficiency and retention is not absolute. A firm of lawyers that spent months debating the colour of paint for the lobby would soon find itself out of business. Commercial partnerships ultimately protect themselves against interior design zealots by pushing them out of the organization. Such a sanction (for some good reasons) is less accessible in an academic environment. This may be behind one of the donnish stereotypes, that of the curmudgeon. Curmudgeons may initially be no more frequent in colleges than anywhere else, but perhaps they can survive longer and rise higher in the accommodating environment of the common room.

There are also organisations that build value through highly skilled employees that for other reasons are not able to sustain a partnership model. Advertising agencies and investment banks are both examples. Small boutique firms such as creative ad agencies or merger & acquisition advisory shops often start with a partnership structure, but ultimately may have to move away from it for reasons of scale.

Of the major investment banks, Goldman Sachs was the last one to operate on a partnership structure, but it became a more traditional public corporation in 1998. By that date it was making pre-tax profits of $3bn, and comprised 170 general partners. At least in financial terms it was uniquely large as a partnership.

As an organisation and its partnership grows, decision making can become exponentially complex, making a more hierarchical structure more attractive. A need for external funding can also be a trigger for change.

Thus as circumstances change the 'inefficient decision making' cost may grow, but this must always be set against the retention benefit. While decision making participation was undoubtedly attractive for Goldman Sachs partners, it was by no means the only benefit of the job. They were also very well paid. It is fair to say that for dons, the participation in decision making is, as a percentage, a much larger part of the attraction of the role, and therefore the trade-offs against retention are different.

The employment proposition for dons

The most senior lecturers at Oxford earn (from the university and their college combined) roughly £50,000, though certain professors may earn appreciably more. This figure may be supplemented by college housing, and dons also benefit from sabbaticals. An important intangible benefit is job security, discussed further below. A salary of £50,000 is what a newly qualified accountant can expect to earn, so clearly academics are not in it for the money, but this of course makes it all the more important to provide them with the aspects of the role that they are in it for.

If colleges expect to attract and retain the best people, they need to offer a compelling package, in the broad sense of job satisfaction and compensation. As we have discussed, job satisfaction can come in part from participation in decision making, from a sense of power. We mean this not in a megalomaniac sense, but rather in the sense of knowing that you can make a difference, that you have the capability to fulfill your responsibilities, and that you are taken seriously.

This applies as much to university administrators as it does to college dons, and in balancing the distribution of authority between the university and the colleges the conservatives risk creating a vicious circle. They argue that university administrators are less competent than their opposite numbers in the colleges, so responsibility should be moved further from the center, so the university jobs become more impotent, so it becomes more difficult to attract good people to them.

Job security is an attractive element of the employment package, but for Oxford it is a double edged sword. By definition it is of most worth to those whose jobs would otherwise be most at risk, and as such it is potentially a regressive benefit, most compensating those of least value. An heroic few within this group might be doughty champions of unpopular causes, dependent on the shield of academic freedom. A greater number are almost certainly the less able, less interested or less energetic. Even a small number of such individuals can be disheartening for their more diligent peers.

Even amongst the diligent, job security for all may not be in the interests of the greater number. A common lament is that Oxford is woefully undersupplied with academic support staff, with 2.3 per don versus Harvard's 4.9[1], and "dons who flee Oxford for America often complain that what drove them was not the pay but the lack of help with mundane chores such as photocopying"[2]. It is obviously poor job design to have highly skilled dons trying to clear paper jams and looking for toner. A commercial response, assuming limited funds, would be to let a small number of dons go, and use some of the released funds to hire teaching assistants to free the remaining dons from mundane work and instead have them do the teaching of those lost. The net result would be the same amount of productive work done at lower cost, leaving money available to perhaps increase the salaries of the survivors. Of course in a world of donnish job security and nationally set salaries, this approach isn't actually possible.

Commercial parallels to the collegiate system

We have earlier established that not all commercial structures are hierarchical, with power concentrated up into the hands of an individual. Moreover the circumstances in which the business world uses partnership structures are very much similar to the colleges' context. This should be doubly reassuring. For academics it should provide comfort that a businessman appointed as, say, a non-executive board member to the university would not immediately seek to sweep away the college governing bodies while renaming Merton "OxAccom Facility One". For those outside the university it should be a reminder that at least some of Oxford's apparently inefficient decision-making structures match structures put in place quite deliberately elsewhere for their offsetting benefits.

If then the barbarians would be perfectly comfortable with the partnership model of individual college governance, what might they make of the college/university relationship? From a structural perspective there is no parent/subsidiary relationship. The university and the colleges are legally independent entities with no hierarchy of ownership, albeit with customer/supplier and other contractual relationships between them (for instance, for the provision of teaching by the colleges in exchange for the flow-through of HEFCE funds).

---

[1]   OxCHEPS and the Ulanov Partnership, *Costing, funding and sustaining higher education : A case study of Oxford University*, February 2004
[2]   *The Economist*, 15 January 2004, quoted in David Palfreyman, *The economics of higher education*, 2004

One commercial parallel is Silicon Valley. Numerous firms (mostly reliant on a small number of highly skilled staff) operate in a mutually beneficial ecosystem with a valuable 'umbrella brand'. A swirling mix of venture capitalists, lawyers, entrepreneurs, search firms, experienced non-executive directors and talented management are constantly recombining in different groups to build businesses and products of value. It is a kind of business primordial ooze, throwing up strand after strand of commercial DNA.

Silicon Valley has had an extremely important role to play in the technology explosion of the last fifty years, and particularly in the last decade, and collectively has had more impact than any one of the large integrated IT firms such as Microsoft or HP. The beneficial power of this group of independent companies is widely recognised. Numerous attempts have been made by various national and local governments to replicate Silicon Valley, virtually all of them completely unsuccessful.

So from the barbarians' perspective groups of small organisations can be as effective as monolithic entities. However, we should acknowledge some critical differences between our Silicon Valley analogy and the actuality of Oxford. The Valley ecosystem is fiercely Darwinian. Those ventures that are not fit to their environment disappear very quickly, quite unlike the Oxford colleges which march in collective immortality through the centuries. Colleges never disappear, and only on the rarest of occasions do they merge.

The colleges are in a luxurious position being both small and safe. Most small companies feel anything but safe—they know their survival depends on constant diligent effort. As a thought experiment, imagine if every ten years the college at the bottom of the Norrington Table were to be broken up and buildings and silver sold off to the highest bidder. What would be the consequence for donnish diligence in their teaching? While some dons may resent the arrival of limited performance pay in their midst, they still remain close to the far left of the risk/return curve.

As we have said elsewhere, one of the attractions of an Oxford fellowship is having no boss. As an occasional self-employed consultant, I've been fortunate enough to appreciate this luxury myself. However, working in a commercial setting that luxury is offset by the gnawing knowledge that there is no certainty of another paycheck. To be your own boss and salaried is particularly fortunate (even CEOs have a board to which they must report).

Another key difference from Silicon Valley is that the university and the colleges are a more coherent whole, more dependent on each other for their collective success. It is a confederal system with common overall goals, even if the constituent bodies may be jockeying for position. The commercial parallels for such systems are less encouraging. While there are many conglomerates where subsidiaries conduct their own affairs with varying degrees of autonomy, these examples are different from Oxford in one critical regard. The subsidiaries do not usually have to cooperate with each other and the parent to accomplish their collective goals.

Examples of commercial federal structures have existed. Cable and Wireless, the international telecommunications company, positioned itself as a 'Federation' in the early 90s, with the various national operating companies in theory collaborating to provide global services to MNCs. However many of these companies had independent shareholders in addition to C&W, and all of these companies thought they knew better than the centre what actions were in the corporate interest.

Ultimately C&W abandoned the Federation experiment after several years, but it is only fair to acknowledge than none of the other approaches it tried over the next decade worked much better at making the whole more than (or even equal to) the sum of the parts.

The prisoner's dilemma

C&W's fundamental challenge, which is Oxford's too, is that a set of individual bodies each rationally pursuing their own self interest may well produce an overall result that is far from optimal. The classic demonstration of this is 'the prisoner's dilemma'. Imagine two accomplices in crime — say participants in a loans-for-honors scandal — have been arrested and are being questioned separately. There's not much hard evidence, so the police offer each of them a deal. Confess, and turn in their accomplice, and they will go free, while their hapless accomplice will get three years jail time. However, if both confess then both get two years, and if neither confess the police will only be able to convict them of a lesser crime, and each will serve just six months.

Now consider Lord X's position as he sweats in his cell, wondering what to do. If his accomplice Mr Y confesses, and he doesn't, he's looking at three years in an overcrowded prison — far better to confess himself, and only serve two years. On the other hand, if Mr Y isn't going to confess, Lord X can walk away a free man if he himself owns up. No matter what Mr Y does, the rational course is for Lord X to confess.

The difficulty is that Mr Y is of course applying the same logic, he too confesses, and they both spend two years in the prison. Importantly, this is the worst possible overall result in terms of aggregate jail time—four years in total, versus three years for a single confession and one year for no confessions.

Often individuals pursuing their own self interest can produce a perfectly good overall result. Not all situations are prisoner's dilemmas (have a Pareto-suboptimal solution, in the language of game theory). However, many situations do look like this, and they are particularly problematic for federal structures. With weak or no central authority to take an overview and focus on the good of the group, the members of the federation can end up with a very poor result overall.

A practical example in the Oxford context is the desire of almost all colleges to be able to teach the basics of all subjects. This creates a relatively inflexible block of posts that may be inefficient in colleges with fewer students, and also make it harder to find the room to recruit to teach new subjects.

Note that none of this is to say that it is impossible for the members of the federation to take a collective view and seek a collective result. It is only to recognize that in prisoner's dilemmas human nature pulls powerfully in the opposite direction. As in some other areas of Oxford's organisation, the structure might work well enough assuming the university is a society of saints. The less true this is, the less optimal Oxford's structure looks.

Balancing the interests of Oxford's constituents

In practice much of Oxford's administrative structure is set up to consider, weigh and adjudicate between the competing interests of the university itself, the faculties and the individual colleges and halls. Any such adjudication between numerous parties is going to be difficult, but is particularly challenging given that Oxford as a whole is under tight resource constraints. The exercise is therefore often one of 'pain allocation'. Perhaps as a result the structure has grown to a Byzantine complexity that would make Constantine VII Porphyrogenitos proud. Reading about the exponentially increasing complexity of the JRAM (the joint resource allocation mechanism, that allocates funds between divisions and the colleges) makes you feel the adage "we need a decision more than we need a discussion" could be a useful motto for most Oxford committees.

The JRAM mechanism is regularly under review. A three month period of consultation on another iteration ended in January 2007. More than fifty submissions were made during this period, which led to an interim proposal, on which 'continued feedback' was invited.[3]

Unsurprisingly donnish decision making has a rather academic flavour. In academe the focus is on debating the unresolved – the purpose of research is to gather facts or marshal arguments to remove uncertainty. Once the uncertainty is resolved, interest moves elsewhere. In the managerial and governance discussions of the university, there is a sense of the same enthusiasm for the debate, which is of course between groups of dons who, no less than their students, have been trained up in their tutorials in the demolition of any opposing view. In the commercial world, the debate and analysis around decision making is almost a necessary evil, a vital but time consuming step on the way to the actual action to be taken, which is seen as far more important.

Benefits of subdivision

A collegiate university will almost certainly be more expensive than a monolithic one. It is impossible to quantify the offsetting benefits of social cohesion that we have discussed elsewhere, though they are no less real for that. However, in secondary schools work has been done comparing the performance of larger and smaller schools. A study of New York high schools[4] found that while schools with less than 600 pupils were more expensive per student, they were in fact cheaper per *graduating* student, since their drop-out rates were half those of larger schools. (Oxford and Cambridge do in fact have the highest completion rates of the UK universities, though since completion is correlated with the UCAS tariff of the intake, in which Oxbridge also leads, it is not clear how much of this is due to the collegiate system). In general smaller schools have been found to have greater cohesion, involvement, accountability and teacher job

---

[3]   Oxford University Gazette, *A Joint Resource Allocation Method For The Collegiate University*, 31 January 2007

[4]   Leanna Steifel. et al. *The effects of size of student body on school costs and performance in New York City high school,* Institute for Education and Social Policy , NYU, 1998

satisfaction[5]. Intuitively it seems convincing that the collegiate system brings the same benefits by subdividing the university of 11,000 undergraduates and 7,000 graduates into more manageable units.

The question that dare not speak its name is 'what is the right number of colleges?' Each subdivision of the student and don body into more colleges inevitably adds a measure of overhead, an additional interest group to be satisfied, another organisation to be consulted and co-ordinated with.

By dividing the mass of students and faculty into more manageable social units, the colleges provide great value. This value might diminish if colleges grow above a certain size, in proportion to the continuing growth in Oxford student numbers (particularly graduates). However, Oxford colleges are generally smaller than their Cambridge opposite numbers, suggesting we have not reached that size limit yet.

Size aside, clearly some diversity of types of community is a good thing, but at 39 colleges and counting, there's no shortage of choice. You can have your college with or without undergraduates, choirs, tourists, teenagers, cathedrals, zealous rowers, mediaeval buildings, Norrington obsession, crowds and punts. This very diversity is itself a problem in a decision making structure dependent on complete consensus. Almost any proposal is likely to be negative for at least one college. Absent binding majority decisions, each college has a de facto veto over collective action, and thus the inconvenienced college can force inaction if it wishes.

Surely there comes a point of diminishing returns beyond which it makes sense to expand existing colleges rather than add new ones? Or have we already passed that point? Should there be an amalgamation of existing colleges? It has from time to time been mooted, but colleges show as much enthusiasm for amalgamation as do army regiments. (The last incidence was Hertford in 1874, founded as a combination of an earlier Hertford College and Magdalen Hall.). The occasional defence minister has forced it on the army under financial pressure. No Vice-Chancellor has been brave or potent enough to try.

The value of competition

Another advantage of the confederal system is that it provides the spur of competition. Several UK institutions compete effectively

[5]   For a survey of relevant literature, see Joan McRobbie, *Are Small Schools Better? School Size Considerations for Safety and Learning*, WestEd 2001

with Oxford in certain subjects, but the university's only comprehensive competitor is Cambridge. However, league tables of universities are not particularly granular and in essence often rank Oxford
and Cambridge first equal. Competition with people in your immediate neighbourhood is anyway far more satisfying and stimulating,
and inter-collegiate competition provides exactly this. The
Norrington Table (comparing exam results of the different colleges)
is closely watched, and is a stimulus to laggards to improve their
teaching. Obviously this wouldn't be possible without the subdivision of the university into colleges with strong community spirit.

This competition is a good thing, though with one important
caveat. It is good if it is competition to add the most value, not to produce the most value. The distinction is between producing the best
results because a college has taught well, and producing the best
results because the college recruited the brightest entrants in the first
place. Competition to recruit the best entrants by offering ever more
comfortable accommodation and generous benefits — an alms race,
if you will — does very little for the university.

Of course for some Oxford conservatives, the very language of
competition is objectionable, the hissing of the managerialist serpent
in the groves of academe. They prefer collaboration with their colleagues in other universities rather than competition. But this is
surely a false contrast — the two are by no means mutually exclusive.
Colleges compete in everything from the Norrington Table to Eights
Week, but this does not stop them collaborating in teaching, in the
colleges contributions committee and a hundred other ways.
Equally, universities co-operate in the Russell Group (for instance)
but compete for applicants, academics and research grants. Individual dons may work alongside certain colleagues in other universities
one day, but be rushing to be the first to publish a new finding on
another. Academic competition has existed for centuries — Newton
and Leibniz knew it well — and here at least the managerialist serpent is blameless.

Structural bias to conservatism

Both a partnership structure and a confederal structure (which in a
sense is a form of partnership between institutions) are powerful
forces for conservatism. This is of course not the same issue as the
'inefficiency' of decision making — it is about the decisions made, not
how long they take. Within a college, where dons will need to work
and eat together for years or even decades, there are powerful incen-

tives not to force an issue and risk alienating a colleague. This is a natural brake on radicalism or decisive change. Equivalently at the university level the ability of a single college to block many changes is a brake on reform.

This bias to conservatism is neither inherently good nor bad. Any institution requires a balance between stability and nimbleness. However, the appropriate balance is partially a function of how rapidly the institution's environment is changing. In the centuries from the foundation of University College until 1986, Oxford averaged one new college every 21 years. The 21 years since 1986 have seen four new colleges. In the same two decades the number of postgraduates grew 92% to 6,768.[6] In the last ten years income of the university has doubled, and research revenue has tripled.[7] Average income growth has been 7% — as it happens exactly the same as the average growth of FTSE 100 companies over the last five years.[8] Between 2004/05 and 2005/06 the university's revenue grew 14%, faster than almost 70% of the FTSE 100 in the same period. In employment terms, Oxford has also been growing appreciably faster than the FTSE 100.

As with other aspects of society, the pace of change at Oxford appears to be accelerating. If this is so, then it makes sense to shift the balance somewhat towards nimbleness. Evolution selects those best fitted to their environment. But if the environment itself is changing, then a higher rate of mutation can itself become an evolutionary advantage.

Dons' role in university governance

We have discussed the position of dons within colleges, and of the colleges within the university, but what of the direct relationship of the dons to the university? Dons are clearly more than simply employees of the university, and therefore they enjoy powers and privileges that staff of a firm would not. For instance, they select, in the form of the Vice-Chancellor, the leader of the institution (and within colleges they select the head of house). In commercial entities this is the prerogative of the board, which in turn is appointed by shareholders.

However, while they are more than employees, dons are less than owners. They could not, for instance, sell off the university's elegant

[6]   Oxford University Gazette, *Student Numbers Supplement*, 1991 & 2006
[7]   Oxford University, *White Paper on University Governance*, Trinity Term 2006
[8]   BVCA, *The Economic Impact of Private Equity in the UK*, November 2006

buildings to Disney to create a quads-and-punting theme park, and
retire to the Bahamas on the proceeds. Owners, on the other hand,
would be entirely within their rights to do so.

How active are owners in the day-to-day management of
companies? The answer depends on the percentage ownership. Both
Rupert Murdoch at News Corp. and the sole proprietor of a corner
shop take great and constant interest in their companies. But 'mass'
shareholders do not. They vote on board membership, major trans-
actions and the like. However, unusual events aside they are typically not balloted more than once per year. This limitation is not
because shareholders are not interested beyond this — if you have
your life savings sunk into a particular stock, you might wish to have
great involvement in day-to-day decisions. The limitation is there
because the trade-offs between mass involvement versus the time-
and-money cost of keeping the mass involved and having them vote
is such that it makes sense for shareholders to delegate their authority to the board for all but the largest decisions (including the
appointment of the board itself).

Certainly Oxford, university and colleges, is of a size with substantial public companies. In turnover terms it is bigger than Aer
Lingus, Halfords, Intercontinental Hotels and Bradford & Bingley,
for example. It is also larger in membership than many public companies. There are more than 3,700 members of congregation[9].
Halfords, for example, has 1,890 shareholders.[10] Thus there is no
question that were Oxford a public company, the magnitude of its
operations and its distributed membership would result in members
delegating all but the very largest issues to the board and
management.

Thus while dons are less than owners in their rights, they are
clearly more involved in regular decision making than equivalent
shareholders. However, dons do have another responsibility
vis-à-vis the university in addition to their status as employees. They
are trustees. Perhaps this justifies a more interventionist role? It
undoubtedly places their rights and obligations on a higher plane
than those of simple employees.

However, it is not clear that you would expect a trustee's decisions
about an efficient degree of intervention to be any different from
those of an owner. Indeed, the prime obligation of a trustee is in
essence to behave in the interest of the beneficiary of the charity. If a

[9]   Oxford University, *Oxford Outline 2006*, March 2006
[10]   Halfords, *Annual Report and Accounts 2006*

shareholder of a public company, the beneficiary of that firm, chooses to delegate most issues, why would we expect a trustee, as a proxy beneficiary, to make a different decision in an organisation of similar scale?

One argument for greater intervention might be if the trustee had particular expertise to offer. The average shareholder of an airline or an automotive retailer will know far less about its operations than the average don will know about the academic operations of Oxford. Certainly in smaller private companies minority shareholders with expertise on particular issues do have a consultative relationship with management on those topics, though even then they do not claim specific governance rights.

Self-evidently, Oxford academics have expertise in the academic aspects of the university. In their capacity of trustees, they have a legitimate interest in (and obligation to monitor) the major aspects of the governance of the university, and so there is a logic for both of these to come under their collective purview. However, the scope of congregation's business is clearly wider than this. For instance, it is not clear why everything from property planning to the details of individual arts prizes should merit congregation's attention.

Agency costs

Those interested in academic jobs are of course no more homogenous than any other group of professionals, and what might be an attractive job design for one person might be unattractive to another. In a commercial context, those who are comfortable with risk and rapid change, or like to be a bigger fish in a smaller pond, are likely to gravitate to start-ups and other small companies. Those who like more structure or a bigger stage gravitate to big companies.

This can be a force for inertia. The people who joined the small company for its free-wheeling nature may be unhappy with the imposition of disciplines that might be an inevitable part of the company becoming larger. The Oxford parallel is that the current members of congregation are likely to be those people more attracted to the current structure of the university than those who have chosen not to join faculty, perhaps in part precisely because of that structure. If you are someone who is much more interested in research than participation in governance, Oxford will be relatively less attractive to you.

This creates a potential problem in that there will always be a temptation for current members of congregation to run the university in the way that suits them best, though probably subconsciously. (We impugn no-one's motives here—such a temptation exists in all organisations with authority delegated by the prime stakeholders). Those individuals who are potential members of faculty if decisions went another way are always going to be silent voices.

In a commercial context this problem is known as the agency cost. Most typically this is used to refer to the cost to shareholders of passing day-to-day management to a CEO who may have divergent interests from theirs. For instance, he may be more interested in running a larger company to justify a larger salary, rather than keeping the company small but more profitable.

There are at least two potential agency costs. Congregation acts as an agent for the wider group of stakeholders in Oxford. These stakeholders are not as clearly defined as the shareholders of a private company, but would include the founders and other donors, the government and other funders, research beneficiaries, students, dons and society as a whole.

The second potential agency cost is between congregation and the Vice-Chancellor. However, currently and under any likely reform of Oxford's structure the Vice-Chancellor is on a relatively short leash. His chances of frittering away university funds on a vast salary or corporate jets are low.

Chapter 10

Arguments against Reform

Introduction

As we have seen, Oxford has a number of organisational features that each have positive aspects, but which also have potential disadvantages. Like any other institution it needs to periodically ask itself if the balance it is striking is still right for current circumstances. Those circumstances might include the level of funding available, the degree of competition for staff, the size of the organisation, the rate of change of the environment and so on.

Equality of pay can be a powerful force for cohesion if funds are available for all to be paid a wage that at least fully values them, and the weaker do better. It becomes a recipe for mediocrity if it means the good are underpaid and leave.

Referendum driven democracy can ensure buy-in and a sense of empowerment, but in a larger body the cost, distraction and uncertainty of campaigns can outweigh the benefits. Increasing delegation of the electorate's power becomes appropriate. What is right for a Swiss canton might not be right for the United States.

In a well funded environment, high financial autonomy for colleges can be a useful element of collegiate spirit and independence. In an environment when cash is tight, rigid compartmentalisation of funds may do more harm than good.

This view that appropriate structure is not ageless but is rather a function of circumstance has the corollary that the argument against reform from history — "why does Oxford need to change, the current structure has served us well for the last fifty years?" — is a weak one. It is equivalent to saying "fifth gear worked well for me on the M40, I'm certainly not changing just because I've come to the High."

That Oxford's circumstances have changed is not in doubt. All recognise the straitened financial circumstances, the associated sharp relative decline of academic pay, increasing and mostly unhelpful government intervention, the growth and increasing complexity of the university, the shift in external expectations and so on. The only debate is whether these changes merit further organisational change, and if so what. We now turn our attention to some of the arguments against change.

'External Council members will do more harm than good'

The effective board of the university is council. As of 31 July 2006 council had 27 members, of which four were external. It is chaired by the Vice-Chancellor. Under the recently rejected reforms the chair would have been taken by the Chancellor, Chris Patten, and the remaining membership would have been reduced to 14, split evenly between internal and external members.

Oxford conservatives argued against this shift to greater external membership, saying that such bodies did not prevent disasters such as Enron and Tyco. This is a curious argument. It is like saying that the fact that a murder has taken place proves that we don't need a police force. It also misunderstands the range of purposes of non executives on a board. Boards are like social workers or pilots - a million quiet successes go unremarked, a single failure is quickly in the spotlight.

Good boards provide at least five functions. Firstly they are an antidote to group think, whereby a closed group reinforces its own preconceptions and suspicions and ultimately transforms what started out as suppositions into 'known facts'. The most famous example is Kennedy's Bay of Pigs disaster, in which the president and a close and closed group of advisors ignored all the indications that their plan was fatally flawed. By bringing in an outside perspective, external board members reduce the risk of debacles such as this.

Secondly boards can be effective champions for the organisation. This is partly because they will have their own strong social networks, and partly because they are perceived as somewhat less interested. Consider the case of an Oxford board member making the case for an increase in academic salaries.

Thirdly they provide supportive counsel to the chief executive. These jobs can be lonely, and a sympathetic, disinterested sounding board can be extremely valuable.

Fourthly they can be a restraint on an autocratic or misguided chief executive. Ultimately they can remove a rogue CEO. One of the ironies of the opposition to external board members is that these members are likely to clip the wings of a rogue VC, which is precisely the scenario the conservatives fear most.

Fifthly they provide reassurance to the organisation's external constituencies that things are being well managed. In the commercial world it is almost axiomatic that an independent board is a very good or even vital thing. Its absence would be worrying both in of itself and for the signal it sends about management's disregard for good practice. Of course some of Oxford's key external constituencies, such as potential donors, spend their lives in this world, and we can expect them to be perplexed at the university's decision to disregard something that is axiomatic to them.

Oxford conservatives object to outside board members, and ask "why not use experts from within the university's own ranks?". While it is certainly necessary for an outside board member to have credibility, perhaps derived from expertise, it is not the essence of their value. This value stems from the very fact of being external. All the purposes of a board outlined above are to some greater or lesser extent dependent on outside members. Rephrase the conservative question "why not use outsiders from within the university's own ranks?" and the flaw becomes obvious.

This logic is widely understood in companies, and many take care to appoint board members not just from outside their own management, but also from outside the commercial realm entirely. This is precisely how academics are able to serve on corporate boards. They are there not for their commercial expertise, but rather precisely because they bring a different perspective. To argue that Oxford uniquely does not need such guidance is to risk being seen as naïve at best, and arrogant at worst.

Those who believe that external board members would be a stable of Trojan horses may also wish to consider why an individual would agree to serve on such a board. The financial rewards would be negligible. Those volunteering for the posts are likely to do so out of love for Oxford, and may well be alumni.

The founders of most of the colleges recognised the value of an independent view. This is precisely what visitors were set up to be, but in a particularly concentrated form. In a sense he was a one man, entirely external board of a college.

The power of an external board member is not primarily in his or her vote. It is rather the power to influence, to persuade and to be considered. Boards are often quite unaware of the impact they have, since much of it is in the form of "we can't do that, the board would never allow it".

Even when votes do happen, it is rare in the extreme for internal members to vote en bloc one way and externals to vote the other. In many years reporting to boards and acting as a board member myself, I can not recall a single occasion when this has happened. The reason for this is that all board members are there because they have the interests of the organisation at heart—what on occasion divides them is legitimate differences in view as to the best solution to a given problem, not some form of competition between insiders and outsiders.

For this very reason we do not believe it is essential boards have a majority of external members. As long as the external minority is substantial enough that it can't be ignored or shouted down, it can still provide great value. Indeed, there is an argument that an external minority can have greater influence than a majority—their arguments tend to be heard with more attention and respect precisely because they aren't made with the big stick of an overriding vote held behind the back.

However we regard the Trojan horse risk of tipping the externals into a majority and thereby ceding control to malign outsiders as absolutely illusory. Given this, we think that in the decision between a bare minority and a bare majority of externals, the pragmatic arguments dominate. To reject an external majority is to frustrate and perplex donors, HEFCE and others with a legitimate interest in Oxford, but equally the strength of feeling of congregation against an external majority is clear. Any future Oxford Odysseus will have to take his choice between Scylla and Charybdis.

'Congregation makes better decisions'

Oxford conservatives have argued that congregation needs to keep control of day to day decisions since it is more competent than the university staff. The Osiris financial IT project and the selection of the site for the business school are offered as examples. It's a fortunate organisation that has no IT skeletons in its closet, but there's no question that congregation made a very valuable contribution in the decision-making for the business school site.

However there are three problems with using this to argue that therefore decisions should be kept away from university officials. The first, as we have mentioned, is that it is a self-fulfilling prophecy. Make the university roles impotent and you will struggle to find good people to fill them. The second is that the colleges are not immune to disasters of their own. Consider the two Pembroke fellows who had to resign in 2002 after they told a Sunday Times reporter posing as a banker that they might be able to find a place for his son at the college in exchange for a £300,000 donation[1].

The third is that organisational design is not driven by simple optimisation of decision quality. While the probability of the right decision is clearly important, so too is the time and cost to make the decision. This is a trade-off we constantly make in daily life. We check a couple of websites to make sure we're getting a good price for our airticket, but not seventeen. We test-drive two or three cars, not every one on the lot. By so doing we accept we may be missing the best deal, but run that risk to save time and effort.

Let us take as a hypothesis that taking a decision to congregation improves the probability of the best decision being made. Offsetting this is the expense of a decision being so made. It is slower, so it delays the benefits; it involves many and valuable people, taking them away from research and teaching; and it is less predictable, making Oxford a more awkward partner for suppliers, donors and others.

These are intangible costs but real, and that apply to every decision taken to a full congregation, not just those where congregation over-rules the proposal. The calculus of determining the right structure is whether the benefits of when congregation wisely overrules, less the cost when they do so unwisely, less the additional time and effort for every decision nets out positive. We are not suggesting this can be solved. Rather we are saying that to argue from an instance or two when congregation has been wiser than the administration is not by itself a compelling argument to retain current structures.

A parallel example of the unusually large effort Oxford invests in its decision making is its strategic plan[2]. I have created such plans for various organisations, and I have nothing but sympathy for the authors. However, in the Oxford context it took three years to put the plan together. For most commercial organisations this is an annual process taking a few months.

An acid test of strategic plans is whether they include "we won't"s or "we'll stop"s as well as the "we will"s. It's easy to list the things you'd like to do, but all organisations operate under constraints of money and time. The hard choices are how to optimise under such

---

[1] "Oxford moves to curb cash for places row", *THES*, 25 March 2002
[2] Oxford University *Corporate Plan 2005-06 to 2009-10*, September 2005

constraints, and by extension to what you would like to do but are not going to. Oxford's strategic plan is light on won't-dos – a decision to slow the growth in student numbers is an honourable exception. In a body made up of a loose coalition of the willing and unwilling, with no process for collective binding commitments, this is hardly surprising, but it does highlight Oxford's organisational challenges.

'If it ain't broke, don't fix it"

Another of the arguments against reform is in essence "if it ain't broke, don't fix it". The conservatives offer as evidence Oxford's reputation, its performance in various league tables, the quality of its research and so on, all of which remain highly impressive. This is an important argument, but it needs to be seen in the context of the assets Oxford has. In a commercial context, you would prefer to invest in a company that made £1m from a base of £5m capital employed, rather than one that made £2m from £100m capital employed. Is Oxford making a good academic return on its tangible and intangible assets, or is its high standing simply a result of an enormous legacy? Put another way, does Oxford's current return on assets suggest the potential for even better performance?

Organisations with such an enormous legacy can deliver apparently good results despite dysfunction. I worked at Hongkong Telecom in the mid 90s at a time when that company had an incredibly lucrative monopoly of international telephone calls. As a management team we turned in great results, but joked (with a certain nervous humility) that a troop of chimps could probably do as well.

Oxford's reputation

There is no doubt that Oxford has such a legacy. Its financial endowment is part of it, but I would argue that Oxford's reputation is of greater importance. It is this perception of Oxford as one of the two best universities in the UK, and one of the very top tier in the world, that attracts the very best people. Because it is the quality of the people that is most important in driving Oxford's success and hence reputation, this success can be self sustaining, at least for a time.

The image of Oxford that most prospective students have is probably only remotely influenced by the current academic progress and administrative and financial efficiency of the university. Things could be quite bad at Oxford for many years before the reputation of the institution as the university of Tony Blair and Margaret

Thatcher, John Wesley and Cardinal Newman, and Inspector Morse and Sebastian Flyte (whoever it might be that attracts the applicant) fades away.

Potential members of the Oxford faculty may make a somewhat more informed decision than the typical sixth-former, but like everyone else academics derive satisfaction from being part of a prestigious organisation, whether or not that prestige is currently fully merited. Consider Britons proud to be of a country that once had a great empire, or was a leader in the abolition of slavery (according to taste).

To what does this valuable reputation attach, the universities or the colleges? Of course the answer is both, but we can reasonably ask how it is distributed. All the evidence points to the university reputation carrying greater weight than the colleges. Is it plausible that someone would have heard of one of the colleges, not the university? Would a sixth-former turn down a place at Oxford because she did not get her first choice college? Would an employer turn down an applicant because they went to the wrong college? Would a charity decline to fund medical research by a don at a weaker college? In the overwhelming majority of cases the answer is no. On the other hand, did Gordon Brown check the demographics of Magdalen in particular before launching his Laura Spence attack? Almost certainly not. It is the fate of the Oxford colleges to be gilded or tarred with the same brush as the university.

If we look at news coverage, we again see the colleges' low profile relative to the university. In the month to February 14th 2007, Google News showed no more than 20 stories for any one college. It showed 1,426 for 'Oxford University'. Traffic to Oxford webpages tells the same story. The busiest college subdomain within the university website (Merton) gets 2% of the site's traffic. This is less than each of the subdomains for admissions, chemistry, physics, careers, the Saïd Business School and several other university departments.

Thus in the public mind, the colleges' reputation is subordinate to the university's. Why does this matter? Because it suggests that this valuable legacy is not the sum of the colleges' good characters, but rather is a common good. If the reputation of Oxford as a whole has fallen, the success of a particular college will do little to redeem the quality of its own applicants (for junior or senior membership). Colleges can fail independently, but they can only succeed collectively. Those fighting fiercely for the autonomy of their college at the expense of the wider good of the university may find that they have simply succeeded in booking a first class stateroom on the Titanic.

Oxford's endowment

In addition to its own reputation, Oxford also has great financial advantages in the form of its endowments. The practice is to make envious comparisons to the wealth of Harvard and Yale. These institutions clearly are far richer than Oxford. At June 30 2005 Harvard had an endowment of $25.9bn (£13.2bn).[3] Even the Harvard Divinity School had an endowment of $455m, significantly bigger than that of any university in the UK other than Oxford and Cambridge. Harvard's total is 4.3 times the size of Oxford's cash endowment. Even if we add in our crude estimates of the value of OUP and Oxford's historic buildings, Harvard has about 2.3 times Oxford's endowment. Of course Harvard has some quite respectable historic buildings of its own. It is also supporting less than half the number of undergraduates.

However if a proof point of the virtues of Oxford's current structure is that it is performing well relative to all the other UK universities, then the relevant wealth comparison is to those institutions. The combined endowment of Oxford University and the colleges is £2.8bn in 2005. The next richest UK university (aside from Cambridge, which has a similar endowment to Oxford) is Edinburgh, with £180m.[4]

Unsurprisingly, the colleges' endowments are an extremely important part of their financial health—funds drawn from endowments (and interest) represented 14% of aggregate college and university income in 2005/06. Clearly if Oxford and Cambridge couldn't do a better job than their UK rivals, it would be enormously damning, given their financial and reputational advantages.

Performance relative to inputs

Of course, the existence of these advantages doesn't prove Oxford must be being inefficient. It just means that success relative to other less fortunate institutions doesn't mean Oxford is fantastically efficient. The fact that my Ferrari goes faster than your bicycle doesn't prove I'm a good driver.

---

[3]   *Harvard University Fact Book, 2005/06*. Figure for June 30 2005. Exchange rate of $1.96 to the Pound
[4]   The Sutton Trust *University Funding – An Update*, December 2006

Can we test whether Oxford's good results are merely a result of its highly qualified intake, or a result of particularly good education while there? That Oxford's intake is very good is not in doubt. The average 'UCAS tariff score' (a measure of A-Level and equivalent results) to get into Oxford in 2002/03 was 512,[5] against an unweighted average across 109 UK universities of 301. Only Cambridge, at 525, had a higher score. If we look at the portion of good honours degrees (firsts and 2:1s) against this score for UK universities, we see the expected correlation.

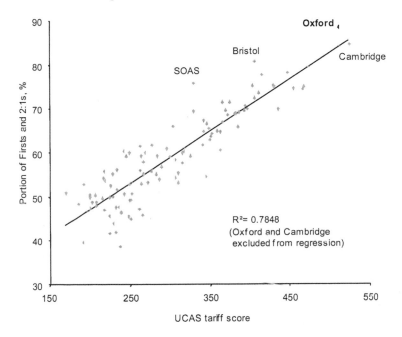

Good honours degrees vs Entry requirements, UK Universities

Oxford sits at the top right, with a highly qualified intake getting many good degrees. More particularly it lies above the regression line calculated from the other points, suggesting it is doing a better job of adding value than most institutions. If you believed that a 2:1 from Oxford was a better result than a 2:1 from a younger university, then you would be even more positive about Oxford's performance than this crude analysis suggests.

[5]   Figures in this section are author's analysis of HESA statistics for 2003/04, quoted in *The Times Good University Guide,* 2006

(We note in passing that while Oxford's intake is amongst the brightest in the UK, it may not actually be as good as the Ivy League's. Oxbridge's intake is a relatively expansive 0.93% of UK 18 year olds. The Ivies' undergraduate intake represents 0.44% of US 18 year olds. Even if the US 'prestige' group is expanded to include MIT and Stanford, the portion only rises to 0.52%.[6])

As discussed above, Oxford not only has the advantage of being able to be selective in its intake. It also has more money to spend on teaching. The simplest way to compare this across universities is to look at the students to teaching staff ratio. Oxford does well on this measure at 13.0:1, lower than the average of 18.4. However there are several institutions with lower ratios, including Cambridge, Imperial and UCL (the last two have significantly higher numbers of overseas students to fund more staff). If we compare degree results to the students to staff ratio (SSR), we again see the expected correlation—a lower ratio gives better degrees—though the linkage is weaker than that between results and entry requirements:

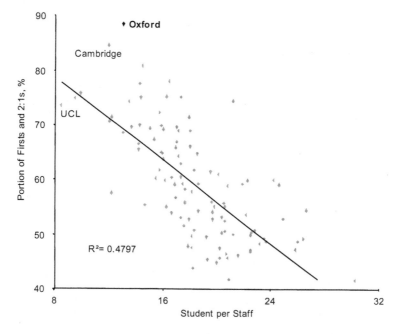

Good honours degrees vs Students per staff , UK Universities

[6]   Author's analysis of admissions figures from university websites, and US census and ONS population data

Once again, Oxford is above the line, suggesting a better performance than the simple correlation would suggest. One obvious potential explanation is that this comparison takes no account of the quality of the staff doing the teaching. We would hope and expect that Oxford's highly qualified faculty do a good job for their numbers.

We have here taken the student to staff ratio as an input variable, but we do not mean that this arrives without effort. While the schools and sixth formers have done the work to produce the UCAS tariff, Oxford clearly goes to expense and trouble to provide a good ratio of dons to students. We are treating it as an input to test whether Oxford is getting value for that expense. As a general point, we believe the chart above shows (if it needed proving) that there are undoubtedly benefits to providing a proportionate number of staff to students in any institution.

So Oxford does well versus its intake and its SSR, but perhaps each is the cause of the other — it does better than its intake would suggest because of its SSR, and vice versa. Perhaps once we take both of these input advantages into account, Oxford will compare less well?

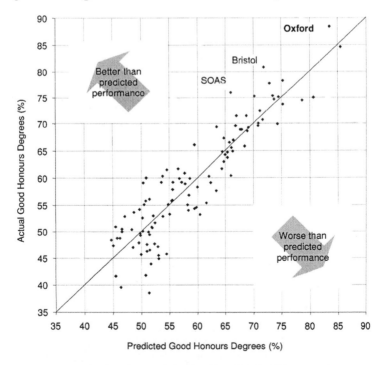

Actual vs Predicted Good Honours Degrees

When we regress degree performance against these two variables,[7] we get a very good correlation ($R^2=0.827$). Using this correlation to predict performance for each of the universities based on their respective SSRs and intakes, we are able to compare the actual performance versus that which might be expected.

Again, Oxford is doing better than its inputs alone might suggest (though not to a statistically significant extent).

This analysis has been somewhat crude. A more sophisticated approach would, for instance, compare the degree results of a given year to the same cohort's A-levels at year of entry. We also have not taken account of subject mix, or the proportion of students completing their courses. Drop-outs might flatter their university by taking a potential low degree result out of the mix. Oxford has an extremely low drop-out rate, and so is disadvantaged by this omission. As mentioned above we have made the conservative assumption that all Firsts and 2:1s are created equal.

Finally, we have assumed that students are raw clay (perhaps of varying quality), to be shaped by a university, but they too are agents. According to Higher Education Policy Institute figures Oxford students appear to work harder than the average student, even allowing for their shorter terms.[8]

However we do believe the analysis above provides reassurance that Oxford isn't simply coasting to the top of the rankings based on highly selective entry and lavish provision of teaching staff. These inputs are undoubtedly helpful, but Oxford is making good use of them. Equally, while we take reassurance from this, we see no grounds for complacency. The analysis shows that other universities are further above the predicted performance line, and so may be adding more value than Oxford. More directly, a common sense look at how Oxford currently operates suggests there is potential for improvement.

---

[7] Each of which are significant at the 95% level
[8] Author's analysis of figures in Bahram Bekhradnia, Carolyn Whitnall and Tom Sastry, *The academic experience of students in English universities*, October 2006, assuming a 10 week term for non-Oxbridge universities and 8 weeks for Oxbridge

International comparisons

But what of the international comparison? Oxford does well not just against its UK peers, but also against overseas competition. In the 2006 THES/QS World University Rankings,[9] Oxford was third, behind Harvard and Cambridge, and ahead or Stanford, Yale and Princeton, each of which have per-student endowments of at least three times Oxford's.

One factor in Oxford's success may be its international faculty, which makes up 34% of the total,[10] roughly comparable to Cambridge, ICL and LSE, but far ahead of the US average amongst top 20 universities of 10% (Yale is an exception at 29%). While there is persistent anxiety about the academic brain drain, Oxford appears to be more draining than drained. The effect of this is to give Oxford a wider catchment area for its faculty, helping improve the average quality.

We believe there are several reasons Oxford is able to attract a good number of international academics. Its reputation, being English speaking, and operating under an immigration regime more friendly than America's are all helpful. As discussed elsewhere, better academic pay than other countries (with the exception of America) may also be a factor. We also suspect that the 'massification' of education elsewhere in continental Europe makes Oxford a relatively more attractive place to come to teach.

While we certainly do not dispute Oxford's position amongst the leading universities of the world, and indeed are proud of it, we do note that peer review accounts for 40% of the weighting of the scores for the THES/QS survey. The other 60% is made up of ratings for the portion of international faculty and students, the ratio of faculty to students, citations per faculty and recruiters' assessment. There are obvious reasons for including the peer review, but it is fundamentally a measure of reputation. Without this factor, Oxford's position in the rankings would drop from 3rd to 10th, primarily because of a comparatively weak showing in citations per faculty. This means that it is bad news for Oxford that after the 2008 RAE exercise research funding will depend more on "metrics" than on peer review.

---

[9] There are various international rankings of universities, none of which are without their flaws. The THES/QS ranking seems to us to be the least bad of the global rankings

[10] THES/QS *World University Rankings*, 2006

So where are we left on the "if it ain't broke, don't fix it" argument? In absolute terms Oxford does well, but within a UK context we don't have statistically significant evidence that as a teaching institution it is doing better or worse than its intake and SSR would suggest. In an international context we have an institution that holds its head up well, because of a strong reputation; a growing role of being a European rather than just UK academic champion; and because of the massification of continental European tertiary education.

If "ain't broke" means "isn't plummeting in the rankings" then perhaps nothing should be fixed. But if "ain't broke" means "is demonstrably performing better than the competition given its inputs", then we're not sure Oxford's passed the test.

Organisations with strong legacies can be treacherous to manage precisely because the legacy provides such momentum that problems can remain hidden (or at least can be ignored). Short of massive fraud or incompetence, great organisations do not collapse; they moulder.

Even if the problems are identified, the comfort provided by the legacy makes it very difficult to persuade members of the organisation of the necessity for change. To persuade people to leap into the unknown, there is a need for a 'burning platform', a sense that the current structure will not survive. Few feel that the high table daises are burning just yet.

'Reforms will damage the benefit of a college system'

Conservatives also argue that any diminution of college autonomy must inevitably reduce the valuable aspects of collegiality, but is this relationship linear? Or are there 'safe' reductions in autonomy that can enable the university as whole to operate more effectively, but not noticeably impact the benefits of a collegiate system? To come at the problem from the other direction, how sharp does the distinction need to be between sets of people within the university to create the cohesion within the sets that provides a valuable social anchor and the basis for competition?

Consciously or otherwise, Oxford uses many tools to this end, including self selection of members, cohabitation, intra-college teaching, non-academic college societies, self-governance, financial independence and inter-college competition (which is both based on and a driver of a level of division between colleges).

Accepting that the confederal structure of colleges is a good thing, we are still left with the question of how many of these distinctions are necessary. Is there an appropriate mid-point between where we are today and an opposite extreme where college autonomy is so eroded that governing bodies are reduced to annual meetings to name the college tortoise?

Consider Macmillan's observation that soldiers have greater loyalty to their regiment than to the army. Regiments have no financial independence. They are entirely dependent on the MoD for funds. They have limited ability to select their own members (certain elite units aside). They are self governing to an extent, but are clearly absolutely subordinate to the army command structure. Indeed a general has far more control over regiments under him that even the most autocratic Vice-Chancellor could hope for.

On the other hand, they do cohabit, socialize together, have the same rich base of tradition as the colleges, and have a common objective. These aspects seem to be sufficient to foster strong regimental spirit. Regiments maintain strong and distinct cultures, and they enjoy good alumni relations. How can colleges be sure that even the total loss of financial independence (a level of centralisation not seriously proposed even by zealot reformers) would cause the death of collegiate communities, when it clearly has not done so for regiments?

We do not believe that total college autonomy is a paramount objective in of itself. For the reasons outlined above, we do believe that college communities are highly valuable, and recognize that a degree of independence is important to create those communities. But we further believe that a lesser degree of independence than the colleges have today would be sufficient to protect what is most valuable in the college system, while also allowing for some of the benefits of greater university-wide coordination. In particular, we believe that the following are essential for the colleges to have real meaning as communities, not simply halls of residence: the ability of colleges to have great say in which junior and senior members they admit, and in particular a right of veto; a particular involvement of the senior members in teaching the junior members; cohabitation and commensality; and the shared social activities (such as sports, college societies and so on). Depth of tradition is clearly valuable too, though it would be an insult to the rich community life of the newer colleges to say it was essential.

Financial autonomy is an obvious omission from our list, but we certainly do not argue for any kind of financial amalgamation of the colleges with the university. A pragmatic argument for financial autonomy is that there is a group of donors who would prefer to give to their old college. If they knew their generous gift would be immediately redistributed across the university, presumably they would be less likely to give in the first place. Donations to the colleges in 2004/05 were £25m, and college costs were £221m. You would have to believe quite large cost savings were available on the £221m through financial aggregation to want to put at risk the £25m.

We will argue however for an appreciable redistribution of wealth. We will also argue for a mechanism for colleges to make collectively binding decisions. Returning to our army parallel, regimental spirit survives in a world where orders very clearly come down from above. Are the benefits of collegiality so fragile that they would be demolished if from time to time an order came down from a majority vote of the colleges themselves?

Chapter 11

Reform from the Outside

There have been many different responses to the recent turmoil in Oxford, among which one can identity two opposing positions seriously contemplated by experienced observers. At one extreme there are those who say that the lesson of history, distant and recent, is that Oxford is incapable of reforming itself, and that it can be improved only by parliamentary action—a new Oxford (or Oxford and Cambridge) Act, perhaps preceded by a Royal Commission. At the other extreme are those who say that the ills that afflict the university are all, directly or indirectly, the result of previous government intervention, and the only path to salvation for Oxford is unilaterally to declare independence, renounce government funding, and become in fact, what it already is in theory, a private university.

Our impression is that few people in Oxford belong to either camp. Majority opinion, anecdotally sampled, is that the collegiate university should keep its head down, and hope that it may be permitted to muddle through with its present constitution. We too are sceptical about the merits of the two extreme positions, but they deserve serious examination and in this chapter and the next we will aim to set out as fairly as we can the pros and cons of each.

The history of previous Royal Commissions has been set out in an earlier chapter. Probably each of them improved Oxford in one way or another. But in each case the eventual legislation was very different from the initial proposals of the committee. In particular, while commissioners were instrumental in bringing about significant changes in the central university, they were able to effect reforms in colleges only to the extent that colleges were willing to co-operate. However, if one took into account the history of parliamentary intervention only up to 1979, it would be fair to say that it produced more beneficent reform than Oxford would have done if left to its own devices. Since that time, however, the story has been very different, no matter which party has been in power.

The Thatcher years

The Conservative Prime Minister Mrs Thatcher disliked universities for a variety of reasons. She thought that universities, like other professional bodies, were guilds organised for the benefit of producers rather than consumers: toffee-nosed equivalents of the trades unions which were strangling the British economy. She detested academics' liberal ideas, and despised them for their failure to control student demonstrations and sit-ins. Universities, in her view, were hotbeds of the socialism that it was her mission to destroy.

When cuts were necessary to restore public finances, the universities were prime targets. One of the first acts of Mrs Thatcher's governments was to force universities to raise their fees to overseas students, making Oxford for a while more expensive than any Ivy League college in the US. The grant-in-aid was reduced in proportion to the estimated increase in fee income. The increase was overestimated, since there was, unsurprisingly, a sharp, if temporary, drop in the take up of overseas applications. As a result of further cuts in grants, plus a treasury cap on fees, the universities as a whole lost five per cent per annum in real terms from their overall budget in the years 1980–2.

In these circumstances, the authorities at Oxford hesitated to offer Mrs Thatcher the customary honorary degree. When she was re-elected in 1983 the failure to honour her was seen by many as a scandal. When, in 1984, she survived an IRA attempt to assassinate her in Brighton, many of her critics felt an unfeigned admiration for the courage and magnanimity she displayed. I was one of those who, on hebomadal council, decided the time had come to put her name forward for a degree. But some months elapsed between the publication of our proposal and the vote upon it in congregation. During that time Thatcher proposed the abolition of free tuition for undergraduates, and when forced by her own back-benchers to backtrack, she made up the Treasury's loss by raiding the science budget. In the Sheldonian the degree proposal was turned down by a significant majority. From that day to this the vote has been held up as a prime example of the virtue — or, according to taste, the folly — that a sovereign independent congregation can display.

The detestation of Thatcher felt by many of the voters was not simply resentment at the financial cuts, savage though these had been.

Dons are no more indifferent to money than other people, but when their profession was a dignified and respected one, they were content to forego the larger salaries available elsewhere. It was an essential element of the Thatcherite creed that everyone's worth was to be judged by the amount of money they could earn. It was bitter when this ethos was imposed at the very time when one's earning power was being cut away. In the succeeding years, if I would complain to conservative friends about the assault on the universities, I was often told "Oxford has a lot to answer for". I would respond "Surely, as an admirer of the Prime Minister, you cannot possibly believe that her higher education policy for the nation derives from personal pique?".

Whatever the motives behind it, the Great Education Reform Bill (Gerbil) of Kenneth Baker undermined many of the pillars of the university system as traditionally understood. The arms-length UGC, composed of academics, was abolished, and replaced by a Universities' Funding Council, which was weighted towards business interests. Rather than providing liberal education and engaging in the disinterested pursuit of learning, universities must consider the nation's "demands for highly qualified manpower". When the Bill became the Education Act of 1988 it abolished the tradition of academic tenure, so that dons could be sacked in the same way as janitors. An unlikely alliance of Max Beloff and Roy Jenkins achieved, in the Lords, the insertion of a clause to protect academic freedom. Dons should be free "to question and test received wisdom, and to put forward new ideas and controversial or unpopular opinions".

Kenneth Baker's Act had as one of its purposes to enable academics to be made redundant. Most academic staff in Oxford did not, in theory, enjoy tenure at all. The majority of university posts were tenable only in conjunction with college fellowships and fellowships came up for renewal every seven years. It was, however, extremely rare in practice for fellowships not to be renewed, and Oxford like other universities was forced to enact new legislation. Commissioners drew up model statutes that enabled universities to dismiss staff on grounds of redundancy as well as for misbehaviour, while simultaneously putting in place grievance procedures and employee protection measures. The net effect of the new statutes in Oxford was probably to make it harder, not easier, to get rid of unsatisfactory staff.

Responding to the ERA put a great strain on the collegiate university and on the system of joint appointments. Suppose that St

Lazarus college wished to make redundant its tutor in Mixo-Lydian, since there were no longer any Lazarus undergraduates wishing to learn that subject. What was to happen to the university lectureship that he held jointly with his fellowship? He could hardly be made redundant by the university, since in other parts of Oxford there was still a healthy appetite for Mixo-Lydian. Did that mean that St Lazarus had to keep him on, or that the university had to take over the full cost of his salary?

Sex discrimination legislation, likewise, meant that joint appointments presented problems for the women's colleges. It would be legal for St Martha's college, a single-sex institution, to advertise a fellowship restricted to women; but if to that fellowship was attached a lecturership in a mixed university, such advertisement would no longer be legal. The practical solution for a while was to offer a university post open to both sexes: if the successful candidate was a woman, then she would be awarded the fellowship at St Martha's, if a man, he would be found a place in a mixed college. It did not take long to discover the flaw in this arrangement: suppose a successful female candidate would prefer a fellowship elsewhere than at St Martha's - why should she be deprived of an option open to a male candidate?

Education acts: more means worse

Further burdens were placed on Oxford in 1992 when John Patten, a former Hertford tutor who was now Secretary of State in John Major's government, sponsored a new Further and Higher Education Act. Nationally, the most important feature of this Act was that it introduced comprehensive higher education. It abolished the "binary line" that had hitherto placed universities on a different level from other institutions of higher education. If the function of universities was now seen to be supplying national manpower needs, it made sense to place them on the same plane as the polytechnics and colleges of further education who had hitherto seen specialised technical education as one of their principal tasks. The polytechnics were now allowed to confer degrees, and the number of universities, overnight, rose from forty seven to eighty eight. Some of the former polytechnics seized the opportunities offered them, and turned themselves into able competitors of the established universities: notably Oxford's neighbour in Headington, now renamed Oxford Brookes University.

The need to fund the ambitions of the new universities placed further strain on the funding of the older ones. In the eighties and nineties, hand in hand with a decrease in government funding went an increase in government intervention. Part of the government grant to universities was now earmarked for research, and the size of each institution's research element was decided on the basis of an elaborate inquisition into the research output of each university. Departments were awarded a number of stars on the basis of a peer-review of their members' publications, and grant-in-aid followed the stars. This was the famous RAE, or research assessment exercise, which has continued, at roughly five year intervals, up to the present day.

The RAE was never popular in the universities. There were some who claimed that high level research was incapable of vulgar quantification and grading, so that the exercise was an impossible one. Such a complaint came ill from fellows of the Royal Society and the British Academy who spent a considerable time each year ranking applicants for their membership. The RAE's activities were not so much impossible as superfluous: the rankings of departments produced after months of form-filling and paper-reading were similar to those that any well-informed academic in the subject could have produced in advance of the exercise. Gratifyingly, but unsurprisingly, most Oxford departments won the maximum number of stars. The news that in one of the five year tournaments Oxford Brookes had beaten Oxford University in history gave rise to widespread Schadenfreude. But the RAE was an expensive method of producing such occasional harmless merriment.

The most serious problem was that the RAE distorted academic priorities: it emphasized research at the expense of teaching, and it led to a surfeit of publications in pursuit of stars.

The first complaint led not to any relaxation of the RAE but to the setting up of a second inquisition beside it. A Quality Assurance Agency was set up to run a Teaching Quality Assessment of each institution. The agency advertised for "quality auditors", for whom "management experience in relation to education is preferred but not considered essential". The assessors who visited Oxford certainly found it difficult to understand its traditional methods of teaching. There is a story current that Bernard Williams and I were inspected by the assessors of the philosophy department. We were asked what teaching methodology we adopted. There was a pause, and then Bernard said "The Socratic method". "Oh" said the inspector "and when was that published?" Sadly, I have no memory of any such occasion, but the story is too good not to be true.

The second complaint, like the first, was met by the setting up of a new inquiry—one of which I was myself a member. This was an inquiry into the funding of university libraries. In the nineteen eighties and early nineties there was an abundant crop of learned monographs and new specialist periodicals. University libraries could not afford to keep up with the expansion of academic material. The rise of the computer had not, as officials had hoped, reduced the number of works published in hard copy. On the contrary, by facilitating desk-top publishing, it had almost doubled them over a decade. Our committee was asked how to deal with the libraries' predicament.

We met in an office of the funding council, and discussed the origins of the crisis. I pointed out that it one of its causes was functioning just down the corridor from where we were sitting. The RAE caused people who had nothing much to say to rush into print in the hope of winning stars, and therefore funds, for their department. My suggestion was not well received, and appeared in the eventual report only in a dismissive footnote. All our committee could achieve was to recommend a one-off increase (or earmarking) of library funding.

The high point of government intervention in the affairs of Oxford came during John Patten's tenure as Secretary of State for education. As a condition of receiving grant-in-aid in a particular year the university was instructed to introduce regular procedures of appraisal of academic staff. Many in Oxford were opposed to what they saw as the introduction of line-management structures. The government simply instructed the funding council to withhold the salary element in Oxford's grant until we accepted the new regime. It took only a few months to bring us all to heel. I remember the occasion well, as I was the hapless individual deputed by council to propose in congregation the motion that we accede to the government's demands.

Oxford under New Labour

Under Tony Blair's Labour, government intrusion has been less blatant and its focus has changed. Instead of pressure to introduce methods of business efficiency, there has been an emphasis on the need for widening access. Oxford is constantly pressed to take more candidates from state schools: in 2000, for instance it was complained that 42.5% of those admitted to Oxford had come from the independent schools, which educate only 7% of the population; while 48.2 per cent came from the state schools attended by 92% of schoolchildren..

Oxford, in fact had a long tradition of seeking to attract candidates from state schools, and by 1965 57% of freshmen came from state schools, and only 41% from independent schools. The proportion, however, was reversed when a previous Labour government abolished the grammar schools in favour of comprehensive education. Given the poor standards attained over many years by the state system of secondary education, it has taken Oxford, assisted by the Sutton Trust, considerable effort and expense to attract from the state sector as many willing and competent candidates as it has managed to do.

On the funding of universities and their students Tony Blair's government has pursued a zig-zag course. It came to power in 1997 after a period of twenty years in which student numbers had more than doubled, but public funding had increased by only 45% and expenditure per student had fallen by 40% (Anderson 177) Labour's first action was to replace student maintenance grants by loans, and to introduce an "upfront" flat fee of £1000. This placed burdens on students and their families without going any way to solve the universities' financial crisis.

The first significant step to remedy this crisis was not taken until 2004.. In that year the Chancellor of the Exchequer Gordon Brown announced six per cent increases in university funding in each of three years. At the same time, it was decided to provide universities with a new income stream, by allowing them to charge annual fees of £3000. These fees were oddly named "top-up fees", even though they would meet less than 25% of the average cost of a student's education. None the less they were opposed by the main opposition parties and many Labour back-benchers. Opposition focussed on the fact that these fees were "variable", that is to say, might differ from one university to another. It was feared that this would create a "two-tier" university system. The argument was wholly unreal, as it should have been clear from the outset that every university would charge the maximum permitted fee — as, with one or two exceptions, they rushed to do as soon as the act came into force.

However, to ward off rebellion, the Act in its final form laid many new obligations on universities to assist poor students, and set up an Office of Fair Access to oversee universities efforts to widen their franchise. Each university had to make an Access Agreement with

OFFA, agreeing a target of participation that had to be met under penalty of a substantial fine. On the assumption that all those who obtain 3 As at A-level can benefit from an Oxford education, the university has been set a target of widening participation so that the percentage of applications from state schools will be at least 62% by 2010. This target must be seen against the background of the government's overarching goal of raising the proportion of 18–30 year olds who attend university to 50% by 2010.

Looking back, from an Oxford viewpoint, over the history of government intervention during the last three decades, it is difficult to say that its overall impact has been beneficial. Most initiatives have had as their most obvious effect an increase in layers of bureaucracy or new institutes regarded by many in the university as surplus to requirements. (A prime example is the foundation of an Institute of Learning and Teaching to issue certificates to lecturers). Given this history, it does not seem plausible that the way to better health for the collegiate university lies in any fundamental governmental review of its structure.

This is particularly so, now that Royal Commissions seem to have gone out of fashion. The members of Oxford Royal Commissions in the past were chosen to represent different areas of expertise and commonly had personal experience of the university they were to reform. Government intervention in the present climate is more likely to take the form of a committee whose members are chosen on the basis of political correctness, if not political cronyism. Anxiety to make sure that every possible minority is represented may produce a membership short on the kind of experience required to understand so complex an institution.

In the light of the history it is understandable that some should think that salvation lies not in more government control, but less. According to Simon Jenkins, the 1988 Act was a deal with the devil: universities surrendered their autonomy in favour of more students and more money, and in return they got the students but not the money. "At the time of the 1988 Education Reform Act the universities should have rejected Margaret Thatcher's takeover bid and gone down the American route. They should have charged proper fees to those who could afford them, as with graduate students. They should have called the government's bluff to continue research grants and give state bursaries to poor students." Instead, they accepted state control and declining standards. Top up fees only made matters worse, according to Jenkins. Writing in the *Times* of

28/1/04, the day after the commons approved them, he said "Had last night's vote been lost, there was a chance that necessity might lead the top British universities to find the courage to go independent. Both Oxford and Cambridge are trading at a loss and drawing down on their endowments. This could not last. Instead the extra £2,000 per student will enable universities to stagger on a few more years, before facing further destitution and recourse to government."

Would it be possible for Oxford to declare independence as Jenkins suggests?. Certainly, in law, Oxford is an independent charity; it has no obligation to accept money from HEFCE with all the controls attached. But would it be able to afford to forego the third of its income that comes from that source? That is the question we address in the next chapter.

Chapter 12

Declaration of Independence?

How might Oxford break away from its dependency on government funding? Let us start with the (relatively) low bar of forgoing the £59m from HEFCE in 2005/06 for teaching. We believe it is in teaching that some of the constraints that come with the funding have been least helpful. Oxford is struggling to provide a business class product while being required to offer an economy class fare.

The marginal benefit of students

One way to improve Oxford's finances would be to increase or decrease student numbers. This is obviously a somewhat vague recommendation, but it depends on the marginal contribution an incremental student makes. Does one extra student bring in more in income—fees, HEFCE grants and so on—than he triggers in further costs? The typical calculations of the loss made per student are on a fully allocated basis. That is to say, they allocate against each student a portion of shared costs, such as the Bodleian, that are not actually triggered by that student. This fully allocated approach is entirely appropriate for determining whether teaching overall is fully funded, but it doesn't help us much with the question as to whether an incremental student improves or worsens the financial situation.

Many of Oxford's costs are fixed—that is, do not change with a change in the number of students. Examples would include the cost of heads of houses, the development office, exam setting, lectures, Bodleian premises and catalogues, college gardens and so on. By contrast variable costs would include exam marking, tutorials, catering and so on. A marginal cost calculation would include only these variable costs, not any allocation of the fixed. It is therefore by definition lower than fully allocated cost.

We have made a rough estimate of the fixed and variable portion of per student cost based on useful analysis by OxCHEPS and the Ulanov partnership.[1] This analysis shows a cost per student for 2002/03 of £18,600[2] broken down as below. We have applied four years of inflation at an average of 3.2% to estimate equivalent costs for 2006/07 (given that some university costs are rising faster than inflation, this may be a slightly optimistic estimate). Note that we are moving to a more recent year here in order to consider the impact of the newly increased top-up fees. We have also made assumptions for the fixed and variable nature of the individual line items. For instance, we have assumed tutorial costs are entirely driven by student numbers, but that the cost of lectures, labs and libraries are only 33% variable—that is, a 10% increase in student numbers would only increase these costs by 3.3%. The methodology gives us a variable cost of £8,800 per undergraduate.

	Total		Variable	Variable
	2002/03	2006/07	Portion	2006/07
Colleges				
Instruction and Student Servs (tutorial)	4.2	4.8	100%	4.8
Institutional & Comm'ty Servs (chapel, clubs)	1.6	1.8	25%	0.5
Admin & overhead	1.8	2.0	0%	0.0
	7.6	8.6		5.2
University				
Instruction and Student Servs (lectures, labs, libraries)	9.2	10.4	33%	3.4
Institutional & Comm'ty Servs (museums, athletics)	0.6	0.7	25%	0.2
Admin & overhead	1.2	1.4	0%	0.0
	11.0	12.5		3.6
	18.6	21.1		8.8

Per Undergraduate costs, £'000

[1] OxCHEPS and the Ulanov Partnership, *Costing, funding and sustaining higher education : A case study of Oxford University*, February 2004

[2] This compares to a 2005 figure of £12,600 to £14,600 for a non-medical undergraduate, quoted in Oxford University, *Corporate Plan 2005-6 to 2009-10*, July 2005. (The cost per medical student would be much above this, and would bring these numbers closer to the £18,600 figure). We have used the OxCHEPS and Ulanov figures although they are both dated and debated, since they provide a breakdown of the total figure into different cost categories

Not all students will have the same marginal cost. Scientists are more expensive than fine arts students, who in turn are more expensive than mathematicians. Applying a similar methodology to OxCHEPS and Ulanov figures for science and art undergraduates, we get marginal costs of £9,700 and £8,300 respectively.

Based on figures used in the JRAM calculations[3], we estimate per UK/EU student income of £7,300. Of this £2,400 comes from the top-up fee of £3,000 less an allowance for bursaries of £600. The remainder of £4,900 comes from the HEFCE teaching grant. The HEFCE portion of this varies by subject.

While there are appreciable margins of error on these cost figures we can see that the total revenue is rather less than the marginal cost (£7,300 vs £8,800). This suggests that even after we make allowance for a good portion of costs being fixed, there is likely to be a net cost to any increase in student numbers — each extra UK/EU undergraduate admitted makes Oxford worse off by £1,500 per year. The income from overseas students is higher, by at least £6,000, and they do easily make a positive contribution. Amongst post-graduates UK students are only 37% of the total (other EU is a further 21%). For undergrads UK students are still 86% and other EU 8%.

The above analysis has looked at the marginal contribution of a student from an aggregated Oxford perspective, but you can do a similar calculation for the university and the colleges respectively. For instance, through the mechanism of the JRAM the colleges receive a portion of the HEFCE teaching grants and the top up fees. With this allocation their prime responsibility is to provide tutorials. Conversely, with the portion it retains the university provides labs and lectures.

With the caveat that as our analysis becomes more granular our percentage margin of error goes up, we estimate per UK/EU student contribution for the university as a positive of £800 and for the colleges a loss of £2,300. This is based on income of £4,400 and marginal costs of £3,600 for the university, and £2,900 and £5,200 for the colleges, basing revenue on the JRAM splits and costs on our estimates of variable costs applied to OxCHEPS and Ulanov total university and college costs.

Thus while the incremental additional student makes a college worse off, it actually makes the university better off. Note that this analysis excludes both the revenue and costs of the 'hotel' side of the

---

[3]   Oxford University, *A Joint Resource Allocation Method for the Collegiate University – Consultation Document*, Michaelmas Term 2006

colleges' operations, and were this to be highly profitable for the incremental student, it might change the colleges' perspective. However, this seems unlikely.

We see here another example of the complexity imposed by the fragmentation of Oxford. If these figures are right, it is entirely rational for the university to argue for an increase in students to improve its financials, and for the colleges to argue equally vehemently for a reduction. From Oxford's aggregate perspective it seems clear an increase in undergraduates would be negative, but there is the potential for time and energy to be spent on the debate because those involved are likely to favour a college or a university perspective rather than the aggregate one. While it may be entirely coincidental, we note that in 2005 the divisions (faculties) have been arguing for student numbers to grow at at least 4% per year, while the colleges have been seeking less than 1%.[4]

Given the colleges' greater endowment, it may be fair that they absorb more of the aggregate loss on teaching than does the university. However, endowment income is not a function of number of students in residence, and so it doesn't change the conclusion that it might be rational for colleges to argue for fewer students.

Potential income from higher fees

An obvious route to improved financials is higher fees. In 2004/05 Harvard charged $32,097 (£16,400)[5] though many students received financial aid. This is a large number, but we know in the UK there is great willingness to spend on education, even if not to quite this extent. One fifth of sixth-formers are in private schools, and the average fees for day pupils was £8,910 in 2006.[6]

For 2005/06 44% of Oxford's admissions were from independent schools[7]. Let us imagine that Oxford charged £8,910 to all its students, but provided financial aid to reduce this to the present fee of £3,000 to a portion of students equivalent to the number currently *not* coming from private schools. We are not of course suggesting that those coming from private schools be charged simply for that reason. There would need to be some form of means testing, and we recognise that is not a trivial task.

---

[4]   Oxford University, *Corporate Plan 2005-6 to 2009-10*, July 2005
[5]   *Harvard University Fact Book*, 2005/06. Includes mandatory student services fee of $1,975. Exchange rate of $1.96 to the Pound
[6]   HBOS, *School Fees Rise By 43% In Five Years*, 26 August 2006
[7]   Oxford University, *Undergraduate Admissions Statistics 2005 Entry*

Fees of £8,910 seem plausible given that Oxford is far more selective, and hence more desirable than the average private school. Certainly the number of Oxford applications has been quite resilient despite the increase of fees to £3,000. The £8,910 figure is also well below the charges for non-EU overseas students. For 2005/06 university fees ranged from £8,540 (maths, law, most arts subjects) to £20,870 (clinical medicine). On top of this the colleges charge their own fees to non-EU students. These vary, but in 2005/06 they were typically at least £4,000. Thus even a economical non-EU theologian would be paying approximately 40% more than the fee of £8,910 proposed here for wealthier UK and EU undergraduates.

Oxford had 11,185 undergraduates in 2005/06. The above fees charged to 44% of this number would bring in £29m annually (net of the £3,000 they are already paying, and assuming the number paying more than this, such as non-UK/EU students arriving from UK independent schools, is de minimis). Unfortunately this £29m is well short of the £59m HEFCE teaching grant.

Required increase in endowment

To fill this £30m gap through increased endowment would require donations of £998m, given our benchmark of 3% draw-down annually (£749m at a more aggressive 4% draw-down, but given expected real rises in teaching costs, conservatism seems appropriate).

£998m is clearly a large number, but not unimaginably so. Cambridge's 800th Anniversary Campaign is designed to raise £1bn, though generally gifts are tied to a relatively narrow purpose—in the last two years Oxford has received donations for everything from Korean Studies to English Mediaeval Philology and Anthroponymy—and it might be somewhat harder to attract funds for more general purposes.

However, an objective to free Oxford's teaching from string-attached government funding is also the kind of 'big hairy audacious goal' that might inspire donors. To fund the annual bursary of £5,910 for an individual poorer student in our scenario would require a donation of £200,000. In exchange for such a donation the benefactor could receive naming rights for the scholarship.

We believe the £998m is an achievable goal, but we also believe there are material fundraising benefits once independence has been accomplished. For as long as Oxford is drawing funds from the government for a particular purpose, potential donors are bound to ask themselves if they should fund something that is perceived as a government responsibility. They have, as it were, already funded it through their taxes. Would they not be wiser to give to organisations that are more purely dependent on their philanthropy? An Oxford independent of HEFCE would no longer be subject to this donor doubt.

Potential for cost savings

Theoretically another option would be to redeploy some of the existing £3.0bn endowment to offset for the less well off the fees charged, rather than seeking new funding. This was the intent of at least some of the original donors — John de Balliol was satisfying an oath "to provide a perpetual maintenance for poor scholars in the university" when he set up his college.

Oxford does not have 'spare' funds — it makes a surplus of only £7m on its 'turnover' of £806m — but it has no shareholders it is obliged to generate profits for, so it is rational to spend all the money it can secure. Hence the 3% available draw-down on the existing endowment is already spoken for, and to make a declaration of independence from HEFCE teaching funds using that endowment would require substantial sacrifices elsewhere.

On a percentage basis the sacrifices are not massive — £30m required savings on costs of £806m is only 3.7%. However coming at the end of more than a decade of increasing financial pressure and consequent tight cost control, it may be that there is not this quantity of fat left to cut. (Though this claim may ring hollow in other universities that have already endured greater surgery). The government has been requiring 1% 'efficiency gains' from the universities for some time. Meanwhile, in the past 20 years private schools, which have broadly similar cost drivers, have put up their fees 8% annually (in nominal terms).[8] Thus achieving the £30m saving might require rather harder decisions, for instance the sacrifice of a relatively weak faculty or a struggling college. Alternatively a fine building could be sold off to top up the endowment.

None of these options are remotely attractive, but they are the kind of difficult trade-offs made in other organisations (commercial and government) to achieve wider strategic goals. However, I started by referring to this approach as a 'theoretical' option. Within Oxford's structure, it is hard to imagine such decisions being possible. Would congregation approve the sacrifice of a particular depart-

---

[8]   HBOS, ibid

ment? Even if it did, what of the individual department members, scattered throughout (and partially employed by) dozens of colleges? Would the relevant college councils be willing to participate in a collective colleague cull? Even if all these hurdles were cleared, Oxford would still be left with the need for a complex and doubtless highly contentious redistribution of funds from where the savings had been made to where the HEFCE funding had been lost.

The sacrifice of a college would be an even greater hurdle. Unless the lamb went willingly to the slaughter, it would simply be legally impossible. The colleges are legally independent entities with their own assets and purposes, and it is not in congregation's, the Vice-Chancellor's or anyone else's power to force an amalgamation from outside.

Earlier we discussed the disadvantages of compartmentalised endowments. Here we see another example of the challenges posed by the compartmentalisation of Oxford. It creates a powerful ratchet effect. It is comparatively easy to add activity and cost. It is far harder to remove them. For this reason we view new endowment as an easier path to the £30m annually for independence from HEFCE teaching funds, as opposed to strategic savings from existing spend. Of course, the very fact that Oxford is structured in such a way as to make self-help so challenging is hardly inspiring to potential donors, notwithstanding the offsetting benefits of the confederal structure.

The HEFCE research grant

Simply forgoing the HEFCE teaching grant would leave in place the research grant, and the associated, troublesome architecture of the RAE. To properly declare independence from HEFCE would require forgoing both grants, a total of £166m. This is a much higher hurdle, and even this does not include the other significant source of government funds, the £71m from the research councils. At the same level of fees and financial aid assumed above, doing without the full HEFCE grant would require a £4.6bn increase in endowment. Still higher fees could offset some of this, but even if Oxford were to match Harvard's fees, and charge 44% of its undergraduates £16,400 (a daunting figure), it would still require an additional endowment of £3.3bn to shake off the shackles of HEFCE.

Sir Martin Jacomb has proposed that research grants could be taken from HEFCE's remit and handed over in entirety to the research councils, thus ending the present dual support system.

"Oxford and the others could then opt to leave HEFCE, a step which would free them from control of student fees and academic salaries".[9]

It is not clear what would motivate government to make this change in funding policy merely to oblige Oxford. But it could be argued that such a change would encourage a number of the top universities to declare independence, and that this might be welcomed by government as freeing up funds to support the rest of the university system. If this were done, then Oxford would be able to retain its government research funding while becoming free of HEFCE control over fees. But research council funding is essentially project based, and a university that was entirely dependent on project based funding would be effectively under greater external control than under the present regime.

The hard truth is that Oxford is dependent on HEFCE funding, at least for research, and short of striking oil in Tom Quad is likely to be so for decades to come. Unable to live without the government, Oxford's room to maneuver will be constrained by the need to live with it.

Alternate uses for potential new funds

Even if Oxford could find the £59m per year needed to break away from HEFCE teaching funds, it is not a given that that would be the best use of those funds. The university already has plans for significant fundraising, for other purposes entirely. There is no question that manifold annoyances come along with the HEFCE grant, but you do have to take the view that those annoyances are very grave to give up £59m per year to avoid them.

Given the increasing uncompetitiveness of Oxford academic pay, it might be that the money would be better used to increase salaries. Pay for academic staff isn't broken out in the university accounts, but total staff costs for the university and colleges was £412m in 2005/06. Thus £59m could provide a 14% pay rise for all, and a greater percentage if concentrated on academics. (Academic salaries represent 44% of the average college payroll, with most of the rest made up by admin, catering and residential staff). However whatever the abstract merits of such a proposal, it would likely be politically impractical to raise a substantial new endowment and increase fees simply to reduce relative donnish poverty.

---

[9]   Sir Martin Jacomb, *The Spectator*, 9 December 2006

Conclusions

Any declaration of independence needs to face up to two obstacles. The replacement of HEFCE funding is bound to require a massive injection of funds from private benefactors. No doubt there are many wealthy philanthropists who would be willing to assist Oxford to go independent. But how far would they be willing to dig into their pockets for that purpose while within Oxford itself there are colleges with substantial endowments that they are unwilling to use to assist the central university?

Second, independence of government funding does not mean independence of government regulation. A privatised university would not be an unregulated university any more than the denationalised industries are unregulated industries. Many of the most intrusive state interventions — e.g. health and safety inspections, ethnic employment monitoring — have nothing to do with HEFCE grants.

Is there an option for Oxford to have its HEFCE cake and eat it too? Oxford could decline the HEFCE teaching funds, and freed from pricing restrictions then introduce fees for all. In parallel it could invite the government to use the released HEFCE grant to provide means-tested bursaries for the poorer students, including support not just to pay the new fees, but also the existing £3,000 top-up fees for a greater number. In so doing, Oxford would be exercising its muscle as an institution that is legally independent from government, but to date has accepted restrictions on fees as the quid-pro-quo for HEFCE grants.

Were this scenario come to pass, the net result would be a transfer of value from the families of richer Oxford undergraduates in part to the university and in part to poorer students. However, because of endowment income, those richer families would still be getting an Oxford education for their children at below cost.

While indirectly Oxford would still be taking the government shilling, it would be routed through students, who we believe are best placed of all to judge whether their university is providing a good education. We also believe that a student body that is paying appreciably for its education can be a valuable force for ensuring teaching standards are in fact maintained.

The prime problems with such a scheme are the practical political ones. Would Oxford itself approve it? Would Cambridge go along simultaneously (so that the price differential didn't violently bias applicants towards Cambridge)? Would the government be willing to relinquish a degree of control of Oxford? Even if the relevant minister were so minded, would he or she be brave enough to remove one of the subsidies to the middle class electorate? Oxford might have to wait for a quite precise alignment of the political planets to execute this scheme.

Our conclusion is that a unilateral declaration of independence is not the solution to Oxford's problems. Better, rather, to ward off any further government intervention by reforming itself so that it no longer offers a pretext for officious meddling.

Chapter 13

Recommendations for the Reform of Oxford

What latitude does Oxford have to reform itself in its own way? Very little, some will say. By rejecting the Hood proposals for external representation on council it has incurred the displeasure of HEFCE, and it has spurned the advice given by the Privy Council at the time of the North reforms. Congregation's intransigency is unlikely to find any sympathy at the level of government itself. Gordon Brown stands in a proud Edinburgh tradition of castigating Oxford. He has criticised the inefficiency of its management, and he once went so to far as to condemn Magdalen college's refusal to admit a young Tyneside woman from a state school who was then offered a place at Harvard. (Magdalen had been the victim of a previous government attempt to manage membership of Oxford colleges by King James II, though the issue was then the confessional not the class divide).

The college was able to show that the admissions procedure had been scrupulously correct, and that the course for which Laura Spence had been accepted at Harvard was a less demanding one than the one for which she had been rejected at Oxford. But the fact that he was on that occasion in the wrong may make him more, rather than less, keen to put Oxford down if he becomes Prime Minister.

Nonetheless, there does seem to be a window of opportunity for Oxford to put its own house in order and to defuse the criticisms that would be used as the justification of any parliamentary or regulatory interference with its constitution. HEFCE has only recently been delegated by the Charity Commissioners to supervise universities, and may take some time to refine its regulatory procedures. The Privy Council is unlikely to take any initiative until Oxford itself lays new proposals before it; and the next prime minister will inherit many problems that are more serious and more urgent than the rectification of Oxford's inefficiencies. In the present chapter we will suggest some reforms that could be undertaken from within and that we believe commend themselves on their own merits and not just as devices to ward off external intervention. But first of all, we list some things that we believe should *not* be changed.

Oxford fundamentals

If a reform of Oxford were undertaken from outside, congregation would be the one of its institutions most likely to be called in question. Direct democracy, many would argue, is an unreal dream in the contemporary world, and it is absurd that a town-meeting of three thousand amateurs should be the supreme decision making body of a modern corporation. Of course, companies have their AGMs; but AGMs do not take management decisions and they meet once a year, not once every couple of weeks. Many people in the business world were shocked by congregation's rejection, at the end of 2006, of carefully thought-out proposals for governance reform. Such Luddite behaviour, it is muttered darkly, is self-destructive: it will bring on Oxford a royal commission, and the first thing such a commission would do would be to get rid of congregation.

In fact, whatever judgement one makes on congregation's recent behaviour, it would be unwise and unnecessary to abolish the institution. Democratic self-government is something rightly prized by academics, and it is one of the things that attract people to come to Oxford. During normal times, routine Tuesday meetings of congregation are rarely more than formalities attended only by the Vice-Chancellor and a few officials to see the business through, and they are often cancelled when no notice of opposition has been given. But if council proposes a particularly controversial motion, dons have every right to turn up in force to debate it.

Rather than abolish congregational democracy, we would extend it. We believe that not just fellows of colleges and university administrators should be admitted to membership: so too should research workers in the science area, on fixed term but significant contracts. Congregation, thus afforced, would become much more representative of the Oxford of the twenty-first century,

Congregation becomes excited, and excites the national press, when it debates such matters as whether to give an honorary degree to a prime minister. But such occasions, and the recent turmoil over governance, are untypical of its operation. Normally, it is a pretty cost-effective form of democracy even if it rarely meets. Its existence, and its powers, act as a powerful brake on any hasty project being considered by the university's executive. Like most sleeping giants, congregation is at its best while it sleeps.

Just as we believe that congregation should remain sovereign in the university, so we believe that the colleges should retain their traditional autonomy. In discussions of the possible privatisation of Oxford, the point is often made that it is unlikely that any private benefactor would be willing to endow the central university on the scale necessary to replace public funding while there are colleges next door to it keeping a tight hold on their own substantial endowments. The conclusion is drawn that as a condition of privatisation colleges should be required to pool their endowments and transfer them to the centre.

Such an involuntary disendowment of colleges would amount to a confiscation of private assets on a scale hardly seen since Henry VIII's dissolution of the monasteries. While it might gratify some present or potential philanthropists, it would be a breach of faith with the benefactors of many previous centuries, and among philanthropists who are themselves Oxonians, such a proposal would probably repel more than it would attract.

Bicameral university government

While leaving these fundamentals intact, however, there is room for significant reform.

During recent governance debates, a major issue has been whether the executive operating under the sovereignty of congregation should be unicameral or bicameral. For most of the twentieth century there have been two executive bodies — the general board of the faculties, which took all important academic decisions, and hebdomadal council, which had ultimate financial control and decided all policy issues which related the university to outside bodies. In 1999, following the North Commission report, a single council was placed on top of the tier, with beneath it several academic divisions replacing the general board. It is difficult to know how effective the new system is, since it has not yet been given sufficient time to be tested; but the governance reforms most recently proposed restored bicameral government, with an academic board and a new council.

The bicameral system is that favoured in almost all other UK institutions: typically there will be an academic senate and a university court. In other universities too there will commonly be a large non-academic presence on the court: and the Hood reforms proposed that on the new council in Oxford too there should be a majority of members who were not current postholders in the university. It was this proposal, more than any other, that caused the reforms to be rejected by a majority of congregation.

In our view the weight of argument is in favour of a substantial outside presence on council. It does not seem to us important whether or not the outside members form an absolute majority. On the board of any institution, matters are already parlous if a vote has to be taken at all. It may be, however, that only majority representation will satisfy the requirements of recent charity legislation, and we know that a majority is preferred both by HEFCE and the Privy Council.

Under the present system the point at which outside opinion intervenes most decisively in Oxford's affairs is the election of the Chancellor, which is still the prerogative of convocation, the assembly of all Masters of Arts of the university. In the three elections that have taken place in recent decades the candidate voted into office by convocation was quite probably not the one that would have been chosen had the electorate been restricted to the dons. Yet Oxford owes a great deal to each of these three Chancellors — Macmillan, Jenkins, and Patten. It would be wrong to think that the services of a Chancellor to the university are solely ceremonial. Roy Jenkins used to compare the relationship of a Chancellor to a Vice-Chancellor as similar to that of a monarch to a prime minister; and he exercised to the full — to the great benefit of the university — the role that Bagehot ascribed to a constitutional sovereign: to be consulted, to encourage, and to warn. I am not aware that any reformer, inside or outside the university, wishes any fundamental change in the arrangements for electing a Chancellor. Some have suggested scrapping the current rule that MAs must come to Oxford to vote in person. But that would be a mistake. Colleges, certainly, cherish the opportunity to welcome back their old members, and potential benefactors, on election days.

The Chancellorship is one of the oldest offices in the university. Equally ancient is the office of Proctor. Proctors are no longer the fearsome disciplinary officers who used to appear in many an Oxford novel. But they have an important role in university government. Elected annually from colleges in rotation, they serve on all major commitees and present the voice of the street to those in authority. A year's service as proctor can convince a don, and the others encountered in the course of the year, whether or not he or she is well qualified for a long-term career of university administration.

A senate of colleges

The reforms proposed by Vice-Chancellor Hood clearly were too radical for a majority of congregation. In the view of others, both inside and outside the university, they were not radical enough. The principal cause of Oxford's weaknesses is the fault line between the central university and the colleges, and this was not addressed by the reformers. Or rather, it was addressed only obliquely, by the provision of significant college representation on the academic board. Initially it was proposed that this board would be 150 strong and contain all heads of colleges; this was rightly criticised as too unwieldy. In the form in which the board was proposed to council it had only 35 members, with much smaller college representation. But this too is likely to be ineffective in bridging college and university interests. Any college member on such a body would be quite unable to commit his or her own college, let alone to bind any other college.

The Franks commission recommended that there should be a council of colleges with power to bind colleges by the votes of a majority of its members. This was rejected by congregation, which instead set up a conference of colleges as a forum for the exchange of views, but with no formal powers. Supporters of Franks regarded the conference as Oxford's equivalent of the League of the Iroquois, which shied away from the binding collective decision that would have held back the White Peril. It has shown itself incapable of presenting an effective collegiate view on significant issues. Henry Kissinger once complained that if he wished to find out the collective view of the European Union on any topic he could never find anyone to pick up the telephone at the other end. Something similar would be said by those who have experience of trying to ascertain the united view of the colleges.

In our view the Franks commission was well inspired, and the time is overdue for setting up a senate of colleges with the power to hold its members to a collective decision. If a power to impose decisions by a majority vote is thought to be too great an intrusion on the autonomy of individual colleges, then a two-thirds majority might be required. This would ensure that uniformity was imposed only when a really significant interest of the collectivity was at stake. The senate should meet with the same frequency as the university's academic board. A small joint management committee should seek to synchronise the agenda, and reconcile the decisions, of these two bodies working in parallel.

Clashes of interest between the colleges and the university should, in our view, be resolved by negotiation between such a senate and the university's academic board rather then by placing college representatives on those governing bodies themselves. Members of colleges who are members of council and the academic board can then single-mindedly pursue the best interests of the university, free from divided loyalty; they will know that the college interests will be fairly represented elsewhere, by the spokesmen for the senate.

If negotiation between the academic board and the college senate fails to produce a result within a reasonable time, the point at issue should be referred for adjudication to the university's governing council. At this point a substantial external presence on council will make it easier to reach a decision and assign priorities in a matter on which—ex hypothesi—the purely academic arguments are finely balanced.

Rich colleges, poor university?

Earlier we argued that the autonomy of the colleges should be respected in any reform proposals. But we believe that there is a good case for substantial transfers of funds from the colleges to the central university. Such transfers can and should be achieved by methods that allow the colleges to retain their financial independence and their traditional endowments.

There is both precedent and mechanism for imposing taxes on colleges for the university's benefit. As related in chapter four, early in the twentieth century a common university fund was set up which derived its income from taxation of the colleges and was expended purely on university posts and purposes. After the Asquith commission had recommended state support for the university, the fund was used instead for providing lecturerships for college tutors to enable them to do research. By the nineteen fifties almost all arts tutors had become CUF lecturers of this kind; moreover, these lecturerships were now funded from the UGC's grant to the university, not from the proceeds of college taxation. After 1973 no further CUF money was transferred to the university, and what remained in the Fund was used in fact to provide building grants and loans to poorer colleges. A system that had been set up to transfer funds from the colleges to the university had turned into the exact opposite.

The taxation of colleges continued, but not for the benefit of the university. Instead, its purpose was the redistribution of wealth from the richer to the poorer colleges. Between 1967 and 1979 some £5m was distributed in endowment grants. These grants were originally seen as a once-for-all- measure to enable each college to be financially secure. But this goal was not achieved, and in 1976 the Richards report recommended a further set of grants "in full and final settlement" of the poorer colleges' claims. The settlement proved far from final: for instance in 1988 the Kenny report recommended a further £7m of (inflation-proofed) intercollegiate grants, coupled with a reduction in the university's contribution to the joint salaries of CUF lecturers. (HUO, viii, 654)

In our view the time has come to terminate intercollegiate grants, and to return the taxation system to its original purpose of assisting the university from the surpluses of colleges. Simultaneously the system of joint appointments should be terminated, and the university should become the sole employer of CUF lecturers. This should be accompanied by a reversal of the 1988 settlement, so that henceforth the university bears the cost of funding CUF lecturers.

An appropriate system of taxation can make it possible to preserve the financial independence of colleges while remedying the distortions of the present system — which, after all, was introduced at a time when the VC of the day could speak of "the poverty of the colleges and the relative affluence of the university". (At that time the university income was 2.7 times that of the colleges; nowadays the multiple is between 2.2 and 2.4)

College income of course has traditionally derived not only from the return on endowments but on fees received from junior members. At present the situation is both fluid and complex. In 2001 the Labour government abolished fees altogether for home students. College fees were no longer payable, and the colleges were not directly compensated for this. However, the government's block grant to the university, through HEFCE, was increased to offset the overall loss of revenue. Potentially, this gave the central university the financial whip hand over the colleges, and it is possible that such was the government's intention at the time. However, Vice-Chancellor Lucas understandably preferred to avoid confrontation with the colleges, and it was agreed that the university should hand over a sum to each college ("the quantum") in lieu of the lost fees. The exact size of the quantum continues to be a bone of contention year after year, and in our view its payment should cease, as part of the rebalancing of funds between colleges and university.

The appropriate form and level of taxation could be determined by the committee which at present regulates the intercollegiate contributions. As in the present college contributions system, certain items of unavoidable college non-educational expense should be allowed against tax—the most obvious example being Christ Church's obligation to maintain a cathedral. No system of tax on colleges can be made proof against the discovery of loopholes by ingenious bursars (at least none have built a cathedral), but the recent welcome increase in the transparency of college accounts should make the system more efficient than it has sometimes proved in the past.

The broad effect of our proposals can be illustrated from the 2005 figures as follows. An annual tax of 1% on endowments of over £100m and of 1.5% on endowments of over £200m would yield a transfer of some £27m to the centre. By ceasing to pay the quantum, the university would be some £38m better off. On the other hand, taking over the full funding of all CUF and university lecturers might cost as much as £45m (it is difficult to give a precise figure, as colleges' accounts, though they specify expenditure on academic staff, do not distinguish between research fellowships and university lecturers). This would give the university £20m extra annual funding.

The tax newly coming into the university should not be hypothecated for any particular purpose; but one obvious benefit would be the possibility of raising the overall salary level of the lecturers.

Academic salaries are not subject to government control in the same way as student fees. For many years Oxford's top salaries have been modest by comparison not only with universities in the US of comparable academic distinction, but also with universities in the UK that have consistently been placed lower in international league tables. This fact has combined with the high price of Oxford housing, inflated by the influx to the city of commuters to the London financial world in search of good schools for their children, has created difficulties for the recruitment and retention of first-class academics.

One effect of the college system has been that money which in other universities is used to provide attractive salaries for professors is used in Oxford to enhance the quality of accommodation for undergraduates. While this may be taken to show admirable self-restraint on the part of dons, it must appear a dubious strategy for those who are concerned with Oxford's internationally competitive position. The comparative poverty of the Oxford faculty is not simply due to government parsimony; it is largely a self-inflicted wound. The transfer of funds from colleges to the centre that we recommend would provide the means of healing this wound.

The Republic of Letters and the academic market

Salary differentials have always been a thorny topic in Oxford. The inscription over the entrance to the university library speaks of the Respublica Litteratorum, the republic of scholars. Traditionally, Oxford academics have seen themselves as equal members of a republican university in which each don at a given level was paid the same as every other don. No one was to be paid extra, no matter how distinguished she was, no matter what discipline he pursued. (Medicine, to be sure, always stood a little apart from the academic republic.) The colleges, rich and poor, adhered to a single common age/wage salary scale, even though the value of perquisites might differ from one to another. The sense of approximate equality was an important element in the collegiality of the collegiate university.

The republican ideal did not outlive the twentieth century. It collapsed under pressure from the academic market and from government regulation. The Thatcher government required Oxford — under pain of severe financial penalty — to introduce distinction awards as a form of performance pay. Electoral boards to professorships found that the standard Oxford salary was quite insufficient to attract candidates who were being paid more by universities that were less egalitarian. In recent years Vice-Chancellors have been able to achieve a more flexible professorial scale: but at the level of lecturerships problems of recruitment and retention remain.

The transfer from colleges to the university of the responsibility for lecturers' salaries would enable Oxford to adapt to the realities of the market while retaining what can be preserved of collegial equality. University salaries should be subject, on appointment, to individual negotiation. Since postholders, once appointed, have much closer personal relationships with their college colleagues than with the members of adminstration and faculty responsible for their appointment, this should minimise the scope for envy and resentment that is unavoidable in any system of individual pay bargaining.

To some people it has long seemed a scandal that since college governing bodies determine the salaries of all college staff, the fellows are both the trustees and the main beneficiaries of the same charitable institution. If, as we have suggested, the university instead of the college were to become the main source of compensation for college academic staff, and the sole source of salary differentials, then this scandal, if such it is, would be reduced.

It may well be, however, that the charity commissioners, in the exercise of their new powers over colleges, will feel bound to address the problem of conflict of interest. A case may be made for including outside members on the governing bodies of colleges as well as on the council of the university. We think that this should not be on more than a small scale. Some colleges already have boards of trustees who manage special funds or subsidiary undertakings: these could surely, without difficulty, be welcomed on to the governing body. Their most useful function on that body would be to serve as the majority of a small remuneration committee to determine the salaries of college fellows and officers. The worry over conflict of interest could thus be laid painlessly to rest.

If the university is the employer of all dons, does this mean that it should have the sole voice in their appointment? That is how things are done in Cambridge, which manages to combine a collegiate system with top international ranking—but we would not dream of proposing such a radical change. Colleges, we believe, should have a voice in the appointment of university lecturers even after ceasing to pay their salaries. The decision which posts are to be advertised should belong to the faculties and divisions. The effect of this should be that the pattern of appointments overall will reflect the changing academic needs of the whole collegiate university, rather than the desire of each college to appoint an all-rounder to teach across the whole traditional field.

Transitional arrangements would have to be made. In the first instance, the university would simply take over the funding of all existing joint appointees. As lecturerships became vacant, the relevant faculties should decide whether they should be readvertised: if so, the college to which the lecturership had been attached should be given fist refusal of the post. When new posts were created by the university, colleges should be invited to bid to associate fellowships with them. The university should decide for each post what proportion of the postholder's time should be devoted to undergraduate teaching, graduate supervision, and lecturing. The appointing committee should then contain college representation in proportion to the time allocated to undergraduate teaching.

Another advantage of the taxation transfer we propose would be that it would enable the university to pay its administrators at the appropriate level, which must surely be higher than the appropriate level for an administrator within an individual college. This would enable the university to attract administrators of the desired calibre, and remove the justification, if there ever was one, for college officers to turn up their noses at "Wellington Square".

Colleges would continue to pay their heads and officers, and their research fellows and college lecturers. Some colleges have endowed fellowships and these would of course remain, but would not be eligible for university or CUF lectureships.

Under the proposed system, the poorer colleges will lament the end of the college contribution system, even though its termination has been proposed many times in the past. But we do not regard the equalisation of college wealth as necessarily an end in itself, and the existing inequalities will be reduced as a consequence of the varying levels of university taxation. The transfer to the university of responsibility for the salaries of fellow lecturers will be an especial benefit to the poorer colleges in which those salaries make up a greater proportion of overall expenditure.

The richer colleges will, of course, bear a greater burden: but this, it seems to us, is an overdue redressing of the financial balance. The element of their own expenditure most likely to be reduced may well be the provision of junior research fellowships. These, like college lectureships, are a common way for young men and women to get their foot on the academic ladder, and many a promising academic career has begun in this way. We think it important that such fellowships should continue to be available, if not necessarily on the same scale. But we think that there is a way in which they could be made more attractive

At present there is an odd anomaly in the relationship between college lecturers and junior research fellows. A and B may be two graduate students in their middle twenties, having just completed, or nearly completed, their theses. They may be equally talented, and it will be largely a matter of luck that A becomes a college lecturer and B a JRF. A will become a full-time teacher, and will have little time to publish; B may research in comfort, but acquire little teaching experience. At the end of three years A and B are each only half qualified for an academic career involving both teaching and research. It would surely be more sensible if colleges offered fixed term probationary fellowships combining limited teaching responsibility, limited college duties, and ample time for research.

The limits of centralisation

Critics of the college system will complain that retaining the financial autonomy of colleges will continue a system with a great deal of unnecessary duplication of effort. As we have discussed, in areas such as fund management and conference sales the colleges are already co-operating to capture efficiencies.

In some other areas the duplication of function between colleges is harmless, and some is positively beneficial. An Oxford with two score different gardenmasters is probably a prettier place than an Oxford controlled by a central parks and gardens committee. Thirty nine chefs in competition probably provide more appetising food than would a single university-wide catering franchise. College libraries provide congenial environments for undergraduate study, and free space in the major university libraries for graduate researchers and visiting international scholars. The possessiveness that once afflicted some college librarians has been largely overcome, and the unified catalogue permits readers to locate copies of rare books all over Oxford.

Dons of course are only amateurs when they are taking decisions about investments, estates management, catering, and horticulture, and even the most bookish scholar is not, as such, a professional librarian. But these days every college employs professionals to carry out the day to day tasks in these fields, and the pattern of professionals reporting to committees of amateurs is standard practice in many institutions and organisations, from government downwards.

Provided that the overall academic and domestic efficiency of a college does not suffer, and provided that no-one outside the college is inconvenienced, it is surely a matter for the members of each college's governing bodies to decide how best to spend their own time in pursuit of the overall purposes of the collegiate university.

There is room to ask, however, how far there should be an external input to, or oversight of, the activities of college government. In the past, each college was subject to a Visitor, with wide jurisdiction over head, fellows, and scholars, and empowered to settle disputes between them. Most colleges had a Visitor specified in their statues — the Queen for Oriel, for instance, and the Bishop of Winchester for St Johns. Some, such as Balliol and the women's colleges, had the right to elect their own visitor. The role of the visitor, however, was much reduced by the Higher Education Act of 1998, and there is now a national ombudsman to whom student grievances are referred.

The ombudsman, however, has no authority over college finances. Nor, until recently did anyone else. Oxbridge colleges were exempt charities, not subject to the supervisory or inquisitorial jurisdiction of the Charity Commissioners. This has been changed by the Charities Act of 2006, but it is not yet clear in what way the Commissioners intend to exercise the new jurisdiction that has been given them.

The colleges have, of course, long published accounts, and had them audited. But the accounts were of an unusual kind, containing no balance sheet, and certified not as giving a true and fair view of the college's affairs, but as complying with the university statute governing intercollegiate taxation. Now, however, they are prepared in accordance with the statement of recommended practice for charities and the audit is no longer a qualified one.

This reform is greatly to be welcomed. Not only does it significantly increase the transparency of college finances to the world outside: it also enables colleges themselves to have a clearer view of their own financial performance in relation to comparable institutions. They are now able, for instance, to compare the performance of their investments with national benchmarks. We believe that the benefits of benchmarking and competition stemming from transparent cross-college comparison of financial statements and academic results (in the form of the Norrington Table) could be extended to other areas, for instance the UCAS tariff of entrants or alumni giving rates.

Governments have taken, in recent years, more interest in the admissions policies of the colleges than in their financial ones

Colleges have, for many years, made conspicuous efforts to open their doors to bright working class students. The number of such entrants to the university grew during the nineteenth and twentieth centuries, until the increase was brought to an abrupt halt by the abolition of grammar school. Since then a lot of energy and money had been spent — with the generous assistance of trusts such as the Sutton Trust — to ensure that schoolchildren from every background are not only enabled, but attracted, to come to Oxford. The collegiate university remains committed to maintaining its traditional policy of needs-blind admission, no matter what fee regime is in force. But numerical government quotas are not helpful in the pursuit of this goal. No one is done a favour by being admitted to Oxford to fulfil a quota, unless fully qualified to benefit from an Oxford education.

Undoubtedly, one of the features of Oxford that has put off applicants from families with no tradition of university education has been the complicated process of admission. The differences between the colleges, and the various different modes of entry into the collegiate system, are difficult to master even for those who have spent their life in Oxford, let alone for those who have never set foot there. A system primarily oriented around application to a particular college rather than the university also carries the risk that strong candidates of whatever background may be rejected simply because they have the bad luck to apply to a college that happens to have a particularly strong pool of applicants for that subject in that year.

Sir Tim Lankester and his colleagues on a recent Oxford committee are to be congratulated for having devised a system which provides a one-stop-shop approach for applicants and ensures they are assessed relative to the university-wide pool for their subject, while preserving the fundamental principle that the final decision on admission to Oxford is taken by those who will actually teach those they have admitted.

Money flows into Oxford not only in the form of fees and HEFCE block grants, but also in the form of research grants, from government, charitable foundations and business corporations. Some of this funding has in the past been a mixed blessing, when the grants did not take proper account of the overheads incurred. Now, however, there seems general agreement to move towards a regime in which no research grant will be accepted without the full economic costs being included.

A final source of funding for the collegiate university is philanthropic donations: a source that becomes ever more important because of the shortfall in public funding. It is often given as an important reason for preserving college autonomy that old members are much more likely to give to their old college than to the university. We have made clear that we have no wish to see college autonomy reduced, but there are better arguments than this one: in some years the university has received larger sums from alumni than the totality of the colleges.

Competition for philanthropic funds between the central university and the colleges has in the past led to unseemly squabbles between development offices about the ownership of alumni:. Solomonic protocols have now been worked out to do justice to the claims of both almae matres, and to avoid the irritation of potential benefactors by simultaneous uncoordinated approaches from both the right hand and the left hand of the collegiate university.

Our proposals will seem drastic to some in Oxford. But we believe that the recent collapse of the university's proposed internal reforms leads to a serious possibility that there will be an attempt within the life of the present parliament to impose reform from the outside. There is a real risk, we believe, that such external reformation will fail to take account of the intricacies and complexities of the collegiate university. Ham-fisted outside intervention will damage Oxford's virtues to a greater extend than it will cure Oxford's vices. We believe that our proposals represent the minimum degree of change necessary to avert such a danger. The changes in university statutes that would embody them are likely to be welcomed by HEFCE, the charity commissioners, and the Privy Council.

Our proposals require no changes of college statutes and no sacrifice of college independence: they could be enacted simply by resolutions of governing bodies acting in harmony. They preserve the most valued features of college life: the tutorial system, the separation of powers between tutors and examiners, the combination of internationally renowned research faculties with the domestic atmosphere offered by liberal arts colleges. For all of them there is precedent in Oxford's history. They merely take further steps on a path of reform which has already been mapped in outline by both colleges and university.

Further Reading

This is a selection of the publications that we found most helpful in writing this book.

Adonis, A. and Thomas, K. (eds) (2004) *Roy Jenkins, a Retrospective*

Anderson, Robert (2006) *British Universities Past and Present*, Hambledon Continuum

Brock, M.G. and Curthoys, M.C. (2000) *The History of the University of Oxford: Volume VI: Nineteenth-Century Oxford, Part I, Volume VII, Nineteenth Century Oxford, Part 2* Clarendon Press, Oxford

Curzon, Lord (1909) *Principles and Methods of University Reform* Clarendon Press, Oxford

Engel, A.J. (1983) *From Clergyman to Don* , Clarendon Press, Oxford

Halsey, A.H. (1992) *Decline of Donnish Dominion,* Clarendon Press, Oxford

Harrison, Brian, ed. (1994) *The History of the University of Oxford: Volume VIII: The Twentieth Century1,* Clarendon Press, Oxford

Jenkins, Simon, (2006) *Thatcher and Sons,* Allen Lane

Metcalf, H., H. Rolfe, P. Stevens and M. Weale (2005), *Recruitment and Retention of Academic Staff in Higher Education,* National Institute of Economic and Social Research

Kenny, Anthony (1997) *A Life in Oxford* John Murray

Kenny, Anthony (ed.) (2001) *The History of the Rhodes Trust* Oxford University Press

OxCHEPS and the Ulanov Partnership (February 2004), *Costing, funding and sustaining higher education : A case study of Oxford University*

Oxford University (July 2005), *Corporate Plan 2005-6 to 2009-10*

Oxford University (Trinity Term 2006), *White Paper on University Governance*

Oxford University (2007), *Financial Statements of the Colleges, 2005/06*

PriceWaterhouseCoopers (February 2007), *The economic benefits of a degree,* Universities UK,

Stevens, R. (2005), *University to Uni : The politics of higher education in England since 1944,* Politico's

Sutton Trust (December 2006), *University Fundraising – An Update*

Tapper, Ted and Palfreyman (2000), *Oxford and the Decline of the Collegiate Tradition,* Woburn Press

Index